FUNDAMENTALS OF Municipal Finance

SECOND EDITION

JOEL A. MINTZ and
RONALD H. ROSENBERG

ABA
AMERICAN BAR ASSOCIATION
State and Local
Government Law Section

Cover design by Mary Anne Kulchawik/ABA Design

Printed in the United States of America.

23 22 21 20 19 5 4 3 2 1

A catalog record for this book is available from the Library of Congress.

Discounts are available for books ordered in bulk. Special consideration is given to state bars, CLE programs, and other bar-related organizations. Inquire at Book Publishing, ABA Publishing, American Bar Association, 321 N. Clark Street, Chicago, Illinois 60654-7598.

www.shopABA.org

To my dear, loving wife, Meri-Jane Rochelson
—Joel Mintz

To my wife, Yanfang, for her unending love and support
—Ronald Rosenberg

Contents

Acknowledgments

In preparing this book, the authors have received assistance from a number of people whose generous and skillful help they are pleased to acknowledge. Both authors are indebted to Professor Larry Bakken for his contributions to the first edition of this work. Joel Mintz is grateful for the fine research assistance of Amy Mehta, Alexa Welzien, and the librarians in his law school's law library, and for the capable word processing of Karen Rose and Jesse Monteagudo. He also owes a debt to the late M. David Gelfand, who came up with the idea of writing this book and made valuable suggestions about what it should contain. Ronald Rosenberg would like to thank Felicia Burton for her excellent assistance in producing the final manuscript. Finally, both authors express their gratitude to each of the members of the professional staff of the American Bar Association with whom they have worked, for their extraordinary patience, professionalism, and help throughout the process.

About the Authors

Joel A. Mintz is a Professor of Law Emeritus and the C. William Trout Senior Fellow at the Nova Southeastern University College of Law, where he was a full-time faculty member from 1982 through 2018. He holds a B.A. from Columbia College, Columbia University, a J.D. from New York University School of Law, and LL.M. and J.S.D. degrees from Columbia Law School. Professor Mintz is the author or co-author of 11 other books and numerous journal articles and book chapters. Among his publications are *State and Local Government Environmental Liability* (1995, with annual updates) and *State and Local Taxation and Finance in a Nutshell* (3d ed. 2007). Professor Mintz has taught courses in state and local government law, environmental law, land use planning, and torts, among other subjects. Before entering academia, he was an attorney and chief attorney with the U.S. Environmental Protection Agency in Chicago and Washington, D.C. From 1991 to 2018, Professor Mintz was the editor-in-chief of the newsletter of the Section on State and Local Government Law of the Association of American Law Schools. He is a member of the American Law Institute and a Life Fellow in the American Bar Foundation. He has received awards for his work as an attorney and for his academic research and writing.

Ronald H. Rosenberg is the Chancellor Professor of Law and the Associate Dean for Graduate Programs at William and Mary Law School. He holds his B.A. degree from Columbia College, Columbia University, and an M.R.P. in City and Regional Planning and J.D. with honors from the University of North Carolina at Chapel Hill. He joined the William and Mary law faculty in 1982 after serving as legal advisor to the administrator of the U.S. Environmental Protection Agency in Washington, D.C. Professor Rosenberg has been a visiting professor and lecturer at several U.S. and foreign law schools. He is author of *Controversies in Constitutional Law*, *Evolution of the Law of Takings*, and numerous articles including those published in the *Duke Law Journal*, the *Annual Survey of American Law*, the *Arizona Law Review*, the *North Carolina Law Review*, and the *Florida State Law Review*, among others. He was the general editor of *Virginia Local Government Law* and the co-author of *Environmental Policy Law and Problems in Environmental Law*. Professor Rosenberg has served as chair or member of numerous American Bar Association and Association of American Law Schools committees and sections including the Section on Environmental Law, the Section on State and Local Government Law, and the Professionalism Committee of the American Bar Association Section of Legal Education and Admissions to the Bar. He was appointed to the Virginia Chesapeake Local Assistance Board and the Offshore Wind Development Authority by the governor of the commonwealth of Virginia.

1

Introduction: Overview of Municipal Finance

Over the past several decades, municipal debt financing in the United States has expanded dramatically. By the end of 2017, the nation's outstanding short- and long-term municipal debt totaled $3 trillion, $662 billion, and $229.6 million.[1] That same year, municipalities issued $410 billion of new bonds, the third-highest annual volume on record.[2] And, over the long term, municipal bond issuance seems likely to increase yet again.

This growth in municipal bond use stems from a number of causes. The state and local government sector of the U.S. economy has expanded significantly since World War II. Subnational governmental entities have been called upon to provide an increasing number of services to their residents, whose numbers (in many instances) have burgeoned. At the same time, however, beginning in the mid-1970s, state and local tax revenues, and intergovernmental aid to localities, have diminished. Local governments have thus been under increased pressure to borrow to meet their capital needs. Moreover, in addition to financing traditional capital infrastructure projects—such as roads, bridges, libraries, and fire stations—state and local governments have also had to borrow funds to finance such nontraditional endeavors as low- and moderate-income housing projects, pollution control plants and equipment, student loans, improving the resilience of infrastructure to symptoms of climate change, and economic development programs. These financial demands on subnational entities have not diminished.

This book is intended as an introduction, for nonspecialist attorneys, to the often intricate process of financing local capital projects through the sale of municipal bonds. It considers the major institutional and individual "players" in the bond issuance process, as well as those sometimes complex facets of the law that establish the "ground rules" for—and some limitations on—municipal debt financing.

The book is divided into eight chapters, each focused on a discrete aspect of state and local borrowing. Chapter 2 provides an introductory overview of the most commonly utilized types of municipal borrowing instruments. It describes the distinctive features of traditional types of bonds, such as general obligation bonds, revenue bonds, tax increment bonds, zero coupon bonds, and the like. Chapter 2 also treats certain more "creative" approaches to municipal financing, including tender option bonds, letters of credit, variable rate securities, and other relatively recent, innovative local borrowing techniques.

Chapter 3 describes the process by which municipal bond issues are developed, structured, and sold. It focuses on the respective roles and duties of the key "actors" in the bond process, from local elected officials and city attorneys to outside financial advisors, underwriters, bond counsel, underwriters' attorneys, and others. The chapter also contains practical suggestions for local officials and other municipal employees as to how their tasks in the bond process may be most prudently, and fruitfully, approached.

Chapter 4 builds on the foundation of Chapter 3 by spotlighting the critical role in the municipal bond industry of bond rating agencies, institutions that are charged with assessing—for the benefit of potential bond purchasers and others—the ability of bond issuers to avoid default and meet their legal obligations to repay bond principal and interest in a timely way. The chapter examines some of the strengths and shortcomings of rating agencies; and it describes how they function, the procedures they use in evaluating bond proposals, and their systems for categorizing bond issues. It also provides some suggestions for municipal officials for deciding whether and when to use bond rating agency services, for relating to agency staffs and boards, and (if necessary) for appealing agency bond rating determinations.

The three chapters that follow consider discrete aspects of the law that bear directly on the issuance of municipal securities. Chapter 5 examines the limitations imposed on municipal borrowing by state law, as a means of limiting an overreliance on borrowed funds by local officials. It considers state constitutional and statutory limits on the amount of local governmental debt that may be outstanding, as well as requirements that mandate the approval of proposed bond issues by local voters. Chapter 5 also describes several techniques commonly employed by governmental entities so that they may lawfully borrow funds in ways that avoid the strictures of debt ceilings and referenda requirements.

Chapter 6 contains a discussion of regulations imposed on the sale of municipal securities by federal and state laws. After summarizing the background and purposes of federal securities laws, the chapter traces the recent evolution of those laws and describes their critical features. It also takes note of the key aspects of state blue sky laws and other state legislative attempts to eliminate fraud and deception in the marketing of municipal bonds.

Chapter 7 concerns the ways in which federal taxation of municipal debt influences the marketing of local bonds. It considers the extent and impact of the federal subsidy that stems from the exemption of interest on municipal securities from federal income taxation, reviews the constitutional basis for the federal tax exemptions, and analyzes in some detail the complicated provisions of the Internal Revenue Code and regulations of the Internal Revenue Service that create and condition that tax exemption. Chapter 7 also treats the limitations currently imposed on private activity bonds, and it explores the ways in which the federal tax laws have been structured to discourage the practice of arbitrage.

Finally, in Chapter 8, we examine those features of federal and state law that have an impact on municipal bond litigation. The chapter describes the types of lawsuits that are most frequently initiated regarding municipal financial instruments. It then proceeds to survey the procedural issues that arise in municipal bond litigation, with particular emphasis on questions of jurisdiction, venue, and justiciability, and issues that involve pleadings, motions, class action requirements, discovery, trial, and remedies.

As noted, the co-authors of this book hope that it will provide a concise introductory overview of those aspects of municipal bond law and practice that nonspecialist lawyers most need to be familiar with. In representing their clients, however, attorneys may well wish to acquire a more detailed understanding of various facets of the topic. We can recommend several other books that may be helpful in that regard.

M. David Gelfand's multivolume treatise, *State and Local Government Debt Financing*,[3] offers in-depth analyses of numerous aspects of municipal finance. It consists of chapters written by leading academics and expert practitioners, and edited by the late Professor Gelfand, that cover most aspects of municipal bond law in a detailed, accurate, and authoritative manner. Another excellent compilation of chapters by distinguished specialists, on a wide range of municipal bond topics, may be found in Sylvan Feldstein and Frank Fabozzi's book, *The Handbook of Municipal Bonds*.[4] This single-volume work contains 73 separate essays, 21 case studies of "innovative and other" security structures, and several other features. The book's essays are logically divided into seven "parts" that pertain, respectively, to the originators of bond deals, bond distribution and market-making, compliance issues, fixed income analysis of municipal products, institutional investors, credit analysis, and special security structures.

Robert Amdursky and Clayton Gillette's fine volume, *Municipal Debt Finance Law*,[5] provides a more scholarly analysis of the law of municipal bonds. It is clearly written and comprehensive in its coverage. Finally, M. David Gelfand, Joel A. Mintz, and Peter W. Salsich's short work, *State and Local Taxation and Finance in a Nutshell*,[6] presents a useful overview of law and policy in the municipal bond area. Although some aspects of that book overlap this work, this "nutshell" also covers some components of state and local government expenditure patterns, the historical development of municipal debt financing, and state and local government revenue sources, which are not treated herein.

NOTES

1. SECURITIES INDUSTRY AND FINANCIAL MARKETS ASSOCIATION, 2018 U.S. MUNICIPAL REPORT (2018).
2. *Id.* at 2.
3. STATE AND LOCAL GOVERNMENT DEBT FINANCING (M. David Gelfand ed., Thomson West 1984, with Supps.).
4. SYLVAN G. FELDSTEIN & FRANK J. FABOZZI, THE HANDBOOK OF MUNICIPAL BONDS (1983).
5. ROBERT AMDURSKY & CLAYTON GILLETTE, MUNICIPAL DEBT FINANCE LAW (1992).
6. M. DAVID GELFAND ET AL., STATE AND LOCAL TAXATION AND FINANCE IN A NUTSHELL (3d ed. 2007).

2

Borrowing Instruments

INTRODUCTION

State and local governments in the United States employ a wide variety of legal instruments and techniques to borrow funds. Those borrowing mechanisms vary mainly by the length of time it takes to pay back (with interest) the money that has been borrowed by the governmental entity, the flexibility or permanence of the interest rate paid to lenders, the source of the funds used to repay the principal and interest, and the relative safety and security of the investment for lenders. In a general sense, the more extensive the source of funds that the borrowing government may draw upon to pay its obligations, the more secure the investment will appear to be to individual and institutional leaders. This chapter describes the most widely used types of municipal securities. Specifically, it considers such traditional approaches as general obligation bonds, revenue bonds, special obligation bonds, tax increment bonds, non-ad valorem revenue bonds, special assessment bonds, private activity bonds, and short-term notes. It also treats some more recent innovations in state and local government financing (often called "creative financing"), including letters of credit, tender option bonds, variable rate securities, zero coupon bonds, and taxable bonds.[1]

Traditional Types of Bonds

The most traditional form of long-term municipal borrowing instrument in the United States is the *general obligation bond*. Its distinguishing feature is the fact that it is secured by the "full faith and credit" of the issue. In other words, the issuing government pledges to use all revenue sources that are available to it, including but not limited to tax revenues, to repay the principal and interest on the bonds in a timely manner. As a result of this feature, general obligation bonds are usually seen as the most secure form of municipal debt.

General obligation bonds may be issued all at once or in a series of issues. Although their precise form varies, they are generally required to be negotiable instruments that state expressly, on the face of the certificate, that they are obligations of the issuing unit. Under most state statutes, the issuing resolution must specify particular details of the bond issue, including the amount, maturity dates, interest rates, and the purposes for which the bonds must be spent. Although the last of these constitutes a legal restriction on the allocation of bond proceeds, issuing entities are generally allowed some discretion to allocate bond funds as they see fit where several bond-financed projects are contemplated, provided that the allocation they decide upon is consistent with the overall purpose of the bond issue.

General obligation bonds issued by local governments are typically secured by ad valorem property taxes, which are usually not restricted by state law.[2] State government bonds, in contrast, are secured by sales and income taxes. In those rare instances where local taxing power is limited or restricted, general obligation bondholders are generally permitted to seek the payment of interest and/or the repayment of principal from any and all other sources of the local government's revenue. Sometimes, however, under state law, particular revenues or funds (e.g., revenues from monies raised by special taxes, grant funds, and revenues from the operation of such municipal facilities as utilities and airports) are not available to secure issuer pledges as to these types of bonds.[3]

As discussed more fully in Chapter 5, general obligation bonds are limited by law in a number of respects. In particular, they are subject to voter approval requirements and/or to debt ceilings, imposed by state law, that are absolute and mandatory. Such debt ceilings frequently forbid local governmental indebtedness in excess of a certain percentage of the value (or the assessed value) of taxable property within the local government's borders. They sometimes also limit indebtedness in any one year to the income and revenue of that year.[4] Notably, however, some states permit the exclusion from debt ceilings of debt incurred for certain specified purposes, such as for water supplies, sewers, and utilities.[5] General obligation bonds are limited in other significant ways as well. For example, public entities are typically required to issue such bonds only for public, as opposed to private, purposes. State constitutions generally forbid state and local governments to give or lend their credit "in the aid of any individual, association, or corporation." State statutes often establish specific requirements governing the sale of bonds, including notice of the sale and the time that must be allotted for the submission of bids. Many states also establish a set of final validation procedures for general obligation bond issues, in order to protect the issued bonds from attacks, on procedural grounds, after a specified period of time.

Revenue bonds share many of the characteristics of general obligation bonds. Like the latter, they are tax-exempt, long-term municipal obligations. Similarly, revenue bonds are limited by the restriction that public credit may not be loaned to private enterprises, and public funds may only be expended for public purposes. Moreover, like general obligation bonds, revenue bonds must be negotiable instruments, and they may be issued in any of the forms that are generally available for general obligation bonds.

Notwithstanding these similarities, however, revenue bonds differ from general obligation bonds in important respects. Most significantly, revenue bonds, unlike general obligation bonds, are not backed by the taxing power, or the "full faith and credit," of the public body that issues them. Instead, revenue bonds are designed to finance specific, designated public projects that generate discrete streams of income, such as toll roads, bridges, tunnels, airports, water and sewer systems, and marine terminals.[6] Rather than relying on general tax revenues, these bonds are payable solely from the income generated by the particular capital project that their proceeds are used to fund.

Because revenue bonds are seen as less secure investments than general obligation bonds, purchasers of revenue bonds often require a higher interest rate, along with special covenants and pledges of revenue.[7] Thus, for example, revenue bonds are typically secured by a first lien upon all of the net revenues generated by the project or projects being financed. They also contain covenants in which the issuer pledges to issue all bonds necessary to finance the project; to complete project construction expeditiously; to maintain specified amounts of reserve funds; to fix, establish, and collect appropriate fees, rates, tolls, or user charges; and to restrict the investment of bond proceeds.[8] Additionally, where revenue bonds are issued to finance a series of projects undertaken by the same issuer, the state or local government that issued them will pledge not to float additional bonds, secured by the same revenue stream, unless current revenues are sufficient to cover a specified percentage of both current debt service and future maximum annual service on both the outstanding bonds *and* the new bonds.[9] Once entered into, none of these sorts of revenue bond covenants may be modified or abandoned by the bond-issuing entity. Where revenue bonds are issued in order to finance the cost of providing a service, such as the provision of electric power, investors may be provided with further security through long-term contracts. Under those arrangements, public and private institutions make commitments to purchase the electric power or other service to be provided by the bond-financed property. These commitments assure actual or prospective bondholders that the project will generate sufficient income to repay the bonds.

Revenue bonds have other unique characteristics as well. For example, in contrast with general obligation bonds, which are typically issued by general-purpose local governments, the authority to issue revenue bonds is often delegated to governmental entities that are responsible for particular programs or services. Because the statutory authorization of revenue bonds is often found in specific statutory provisions that pertain to such issuing entities as housing authorities, building commissions, water authorities, and pollution control boards, the specific requirements for one type of revenue bond issue frequently differ from those for other types of revenue bonds. In addition, as a result of the prevailing judicial interpretations of state constitutional and statutory debt ceilings, revenue bonds are often exempt from debt ceilings and similar limitations on debt financing. Applying a principle known as the "special funds doctrine," state courts tend to construe the term "debt" as including only governmental obligations that are payable from the general taxing power. In contrast, obligations that must be paid solely from funds other than general taxes (i.e., so-called "special funds") are not judicially defined as debts. Thus, to the advantage of revenue bond–issuing bodies, such borrowing instruments are legally exempt from debt financing limitations.

One rather specialized type of revenue bond is known as the *non-ad valorem bond*. This is an instrument secured by the issuer's pledge to budget and appropriate the debt service on those bonds annually to a special fund from "all legally available non *ad valorem* revenues" such as local sales taxes, user fees, personal and corporate income taxes, fines, license fees, and the like.[10] This sort of bond usually allows the issuer to avoid state debt ceiling and voter approval requirements because, without a pledge of the ad valorem taxing power, these bonds are not deemed to constitute general obligations.[11] At the same time, however, buyers of non-ad valorem revenue bonds usually demand a higher rate of interest since such bonds carry greater investment risks than do instruments backed by the issuer's full faith and credit.

Another municipal security that is also not generally subject to debt limitations, and that also does not typically require voter approval, is the *special assessment bond*.[12] This instrument is payable from assessments levied on property that is or will be specially benefitted by a public improvement (e.g., a road, a park, a storm drain, or a guard gate) located near the property. In some instances, special assessment securities are referred to as "double barreled," meaning that their issuer may pledge its general credit to provide bondholders with additional security. Such pledges are made relatively rarely, however, by governments that issue special assessment bonds, and most such bonds are backed by special assessment monies alone. Typically, the amounts of special assessments are determined by the cost of the public improvements that they result in. However, a minority of states require that special assessments be allocated among affected property owners based solely upon the value that the financed improvements add (or will add) to their property.[13] In any event, however, once special assessments have been allocated, they constitute an enforceable lien on the property assessed.

Special obligation (or *special tax*) bonds are a borrowing instrument that combines the legal attributes of general obligation bonds and revenue bonds. These bonds are payable from a special tax levy of proven collectibility, and they are typically used to finance either a particular type of project (e.g., a highway project) or a diverse set of projects in a well-defined geographical area.[14] Holders of special obligation bonds are entitled to hold a lien on all specific revenues (e.g., gasoline use taxes) that have been pledged by the issuer to support the bonds. Additionally, as further security for such bondholders, the issuer may choose to pledge its general credit or other tax revenues. Where that occurs, the bonds (which are then referred to as "double barreled") become subject to state-imposed debt ceilings on the issuance of general obligation bonds as well as voter approval requirements.[15]

A *tax increment bond* is a specialized form of special tax bond that is used to promote a single target development in a particular defined area (e.g., an urban renewal project in a deteriorating neighborhood). Tax increment bonds are payable solely from the incremental ad valorem tax revenues that the local government will receive when the redeveloped property in the designated area increases in value. However, limitations imposed under the federal Tax Reform Act of 1986 have greatly limited the ability of state or local governments to issue tax-exempt tax increment bonds for purposes of urban redevelopment.[16]

A different type of borrowing instrument that has traditionally been used by local governments for long-term financing is the *private activity bond.* These bonds are issued by local governments for the benefit of a private entity (e.g., the owner of an industrial or commercial facility) or else to finance projects that provide some public benefit and also have some private involvement.[17] Arrangements between public issuers and private users to implement projects financed by private activity bonds take many forms. Under one common arrangement, known as *lease-financing*, a public entity issues bonds to construct a plant or commercial facility for a private entity whose presence in the community it wishes to attract or induce. The governmental bond issuer then leaves the facility that it has constructed with bond proceeds to the private enterprise, at a rental price that covers the debt service on the bonds. Because of their potential to attract jobs and increase the economic base of communities, these instruments became especially popular with local governments in the 1960s and 1970s. They were, however, the subject of sharp criticism from those who questioned their job development potential and noted the risk that the private entities on whose profitability the security of these bonds was dependent might incur losses or go out of business entirely, saddling the bond-issuing government with financial difficulties, along with a facility of little or no remaining utility. In response to these critics, as discussed in Chapter 7, the federal Internal Revenue Code was amended in 1986 to restrict dramatically the tax exemptions available for private activity bond funding. As a result, the use of private activity bonds has declined significantly in the past three decades. Nonetheless, a number of local projects—from hazardous waste incineration facilities to publicly owned docks and airports—are still financed through this mechanism.[18]

Another form of bond, which became popular in the 1960s and 1970s, is the *moral obligation bond*. These instruments are essentially revenue bonds, in which payment is primarily based upon a pledge of revenues from the enterprise or project for which the bonds are sold. They differ from typical revenue bonds, however, in that the issuing entity makes additional representations in order to satisfy the investment community that the bonds will be repaid with interest. Although the issuer does not legally bind itself to repay any deficiencies in the principal or interest accounts from its general tax revenues, it promises to "give consideration" to using such revenues should repayment shortfalls arise. Those promises are then considered to be "moral obligations" of the issuer. Moral obligation bonds are often sold at lower interest rates than other revenue bonds because the bond issuer's moral obligation to repay gives the appearance of decreasing any risk of loss for bondholders. Those bonds have been criticized, however, as mere "sales gimmicks" that provide a false sense of security to investors, since there remains the danger that moral obligation pledges might not be honored in the future. Proposals have thus been advanced to restrict or prohibit their use.

A *zero coupon bond* is another type of municipal borrowing mechanism. It is a long-term security, sold at a substantial discount, that pays no interest to the bondholder during the period that the bond is outstanding. At maturity, however, the full principal of the bond is repaid, together with accrued interest. These instruments have advantages for both issuers and bondholders. Issuers are often able to issue them at lower net borrowing costs. Conversely, buyers may purchase them in order to lock in relatively high compound interest rates.[19] On the other hand, however, zero coupon bonds also have one serious disadvantage to their issuer: the issuer must sell a large principal amount of zero coupon bonds in order to make up for the fact that their sale results in a low amount of dollars. As a result, some state and local governments issue "compound interest bonds," a variant of zero coupon bonds. Those securities are issued at par (i.e., at the face value of the bond certificate), rather than at a discount price. The value of the bond increases every year by the amount of the compounded accrued interest (which is compounded semi-annually but paid only upon maturity or redemption of the bond).[20]

Thus far in this chapter, we have considered municipal borrowing instruments that are used for purposes of long-term financing. As a general rule, the principal on these bonds is not due for repayment for a period of at least ten years. In fact, in most cases the bond need not be completely repaid for 20 to 40 years. However, local governments sometimes also sell *short-term notes*. These notes serve to bridge gaps between the periodic collection of governmental revenues (through taxes, fines, fees, etc.) and the more pressing spending demands placed upon local governments. In effect, they are a means of smoothing out and maintaining local governmental cash flows.[21]

There are three main types of state and local government notes: *tax anticipation notes* (TANs), *revenue anticipation notes* (RANs), and *bond anticipation notes* (BANs). TANs are used in anticipation of the receipt of ad valorem property taxes, or some other form of local taxes. RANs are issued in anticipation of the receipt of sales taxes, rents, fees, charges, and other revenues other than real estate taxes. BANs are often issued to provide short-term financing for public projects during their design and construction. When permanent financing for those projects is issued, the BANs are paid from the proceeds of that financing.[22]

Short-term notes are normally made payable within the current fiscal year. Thus, from the issuer's standpoint, it may be advisable for such notes to mature at or shortly after the point in time at which monies will come available for issuers to pay the notes or support the issuance of new notes to pay the outstanding issue. As will be discussed further shortly, with respect to creative borrowing techniques, at least in some states concepts used in issuing traditional short-term municipal notes may also be employed in governmental "commercial paper programs." Short-term notes are issued by local governments or their agents continuously and "rolled over" at maturity. This allows municipal issuers to fund temporary cash shortages (and/or initial construction costs) while they await long-term financing.[23]

Notwithstanding their advantages to local governments, short-term notes can lead to municipal credit abuse and financial distress. Where short-term loans are repeatedly repaid with the proceeds of new short-term loans of a similar type, municipal debtors may be permitted to postpone the date of final payment of the monies they have borrowed on an indefinite basis. Regrettably, local governments may then succumb to the temptation to become dependent on this rollover of short-term debts as a means of financing a significant part of their operating expenses. However, to the extent that lenders lose confidence in the local government's ultimate ability to repay their debts, those lenders may well refuse to roll over the notes in question. In extreme cases, this situation may lead to municipal loan defaults and fiscal crises.[24]

Local government entities who wish to make their securities more attractive to investors frequently purchase *bond insurance policies* from insurance companies. The premiums on these policies are typically payable in full at the time of the issuance of the bonds. They generally cover the cost of bond principal and interest, as well as mandatory payments that must be made to "sinking funds" (i.e., pools of money set aside from taxes or other revenue sources for the purpose of repaying debt obligations). Bond insurance policies are sometimes used as a substitute for reserve funds, which are otherwise required where revenue bonds are issued. They may also prevent debt service payments from being treated as avoidable preferences where a bond-issuing local government has sought bankruptcy protection.[25]

Creative State and Local Financing

In borrowing money to pay for capital and operating expenditures, state and local governments often have varying needs for funds as their internal circumstances change. At the same time, borrowing governmental entities face constantly shifting conditions in relevant financial markets as well as in the general economies of their states, the nation, and the globe. To accommodate to this environment of pervasive internal and external variability, in recent years a number of state and local governments have adapted various "creative" forms of debt instruments from the private sector to public-sector needs and uses. These innovative instruments attempt to shift certain interest-rate risks from creditors to borrowers. They sometimes shift credit-related risks to third parties to enhance borrowers' creditworthiness. In some instances, they also increase the types of returns available to investors; and, at times, they attempt to appeal to the specialized needs and requirements of certain investor groups.[26] This section considers the nature and use of those new debt instruments, which we have referred to as "creative financing," by local governments. In particular, we shall examine state and local letters of credit and collateralized guarantees, bonds with warrants, tender option bonds, variable rate securities, zero coupon bonds, bond pools, and taxable bonds.[27]

One technique for reducing the risk to investors, as well as interest expenses to borrowers, is to accompany bond issues with *letters of credit*, issued by banks and other financial institutions, that secure full and timely payment of the bonds. Similarly, bonds may be supported by third-party pledges of collateral and other guarantees.[28] Letters of credit are typically issued for specified periods of three to ten years. They must be limited in amount, payable upon presentation of specified documents by bondholders or their collective representatives, and supported by an unqualified obligation by the issuer to reimburse the bank for any payments made under the letter of credit. If a letter of credit is not renewed or replaced prior to the expiration of an accompanying bond issue, prepayment of the issue to the bondholder is generally required.[29]

As mentioned previously in the discussion of traditional short-term notes, *tax-exempt commercial paper* is a short-term governmental obligation that is refunded with the proceeds of newly issued commercial paper obligations. Like short-term notes, this instrument is typically used to finance seasonal government borrowing needs or long-term capital expenditures in anticipation of the issuance of long-term bonds. Commercial paper obligations may be issued for as short a period as one to three days, or for as long as 270 days. However, typically such obligations mature in between 60 and 90 days. Commercial paper programs are generally structured so that the issuer sets a yield and term for each newly issued obligation—and then issues, sells, and delivers the new obligation—on the same day that the prior obligation matures. To assure the liquidity of the government's borrowing program, commercial paper is commonly secured by a bank letter of credit or line of credit.[30]

Another creative financing technique is the issuance of *bonds with warrants* that permit bondholders to purchase additional bonds at a fixed price for a specified period. These bonds are often made refundable on the date the warrants may be exercised. Purchasers are thus assured a minimum investment return on future funds. Moreover, issuers are able to sell the original bond issue at lower interest costs than they could otherwise have obtained.[31] Notably, however, bonds with warrants may carry significant risks for both issuers and bondholders. If warrants are exercised after a period in which interest rates have declined sharply, issuers may incur substantially higher borrowing costs. On the other hand, where interest rates rise above the interest rates on the covered bonds, the warrants will be of no use to bondholders.[32]

Tender option (or *put option*) bonds are long-term securities, the holder of which may tender (or "put") the bond to the issuer (or a third party) for payment in full, after a specified period of time (usually from five to ten years after the issuance date or annually thereafter). These bonds allow issuers to reduce the interest rates they must pay. They also permit bondholders an opportunity to reassess their investments in light of market conditions, and to search for and make investments in instruments that will yield them greater return. Tender option bonds are generally supported by a bank letter of credit, a credit line, or a similar instrument for the protection of bondholders.[33]

Variable rate (or *floating rate*) *securities* are bond issues that place the risk of interest rate increases on the bond issuer, while allowing it to benefit when interest rates go down. Variable rate bonds generally provide that investors may "put" the securities at particular times, for a stated purchase price; and they are typically secured by a bank letter of credit. Variable rate securities are structured in a variety of ways. Some may specify for maximum and minimum interest rates. Others may bear a fixed interest rate for a specified period and then bear variable rates. The interest rate on these bonds may be fixed by reference to a public index of tax-exempt securities, the interest on certain federal obligations, or a bank's prime interest rate. Variable interest rates, however, are usually set by a remarketing agent at a rate that is below par in the market (i.e., discounted to a price below that of their face value, yet necessary to sell the obligations).[34]

Pooling of tax-exempt bonds is one innovative technique that is used to market securities that could not otherwise have been marketed because they are too small to market individually, or because they are issued by governmental units that lack market recognition.[35] Typically, the credit of the pool as a whole is enhanced and made marketable by letters of credit, the use of collateral, past obligations, bond insurance, and/or credit provided by a state for the benefit of local borrowers. Additionally, state bond pools issue bonds that sometimes provide funds to lend to local governments within the state.

Finally, since the mid-1980s, some state and local governments have marketed *taxable municipal obligations*. This is especially true with regard to the financing of public housing and industrial development. Taxable bonds typically carry higher interest rates than do tax-exempt bonds.[36] However, taxable municipal bonds tend to have lower interest rates than comparable corporate securities do. That is because the former are usually exempt from state or local income taxes in the issuing state. In addition, state or local governmental property that is financed with taxable bonds often is exempt from local property taxes and/or state sales taxes.[37]

Insuring against Natural Disasters: Catastrophe, Disaster, and Resilience Bonds

In recent years, local governments have faced increased risks from natural disasters such as floods, wildfires, severe storms, earthquakes, and similar catastrophic events. To insure against the calamitous financial consequences of these disasters, many communities and the firms that insure them have benefitted from *catastrophe bonds*, a risk-linked security that effectively transfers the risks of natural disasters from bond issuers to investors.[38] Catastrophe bonds, which were initially developed in the 1990s following Hurricane Andrew in Florida and the Northridge earthquake in California, are intended to alleviate some of the risks that insurance and reinsurance companies can face if there are major damages from a catastrophe that the company cannot cover from its invested premiums.

Under this mechanism, companies that insure municipalities and private parties typically issue catastrophe bonds through an investment bank. The bank sells these bonds to large institutional investors, such as asset managers and hedge funds, usually with a maturity period of less than three years. If no catastrophe occurs before the bond matures, the investors' principal is returned to them and they also earn a return on their investment, in a previously agreed-upon amount, in the form of a coupon. However, in the event a catastrophe occurs before the bond has matured, the bond essentially defaults. The initially invested principal contributed by the investors is transferred to the sponsoring insurance or reinsurance company to pay the disaster-related claims of its policyholders. Moreover, the investors forgo any additional profit on their investment.[39]

Employing a related concept, in a number of instances the U.S. Congress has authorized state and local governments to issue tax-exempt *disaster bonds*. These are debt instruments that direct private-sector monies into communities that are recovering from catastrophic events.

Like tax-exempt municipal bonds, some or all federal taxes are waived for disaster bonds. State and local governments usually serve as conduits for the bond proceeds. They pass along the tax advantages of the disaster bond to investors while distributing payments to claimant organizations such as utility companies and hospitals that have suffered disaster losses.[40]

Very clearly, severe weather events resulting from global climate change have increasingly left local governments in the United States unprepared (and underinsured) for the often devastating financial consequences that those events create. A number of older communities, with aging and already failing infrastructure, are particularly vulnerable to climate change risks. In response to these challenging circumstances, a new financial instrument, the *resilience bond*, has been developed. This is a debt instrument that links the insurance coverage that localities can already purchase with capital investments in resilient infrastructure—such as seawalls, elevated roads, improved drainage structures, and the like—that tends to reduce the potential for large losses from crippling disasters.[41]

Just as quitting smoking lowers the cost of life insurance, the construction of resilient infrastructure that helps lower the risks from disasters decreases local governmental insurance premiums. Resilience bonds are designed to capture these insurance savings and channel them to local communities in the form of rebates to be invested in resilient infrastructure projects.[42]

Insuring against Bond Defaults: Credit Default Swaps and the Financial Crisis of 2008

Credit default swaps (CDCs) are contracts that are intended to guarantee holders of municipal (and/or other) bonds against the unlikely—but potentially devastating—possibility of bond defaults.[43] These instruments work like insurance policies. Sellers of CDCs—usually banks, insurance companies, or hedge funds—agree to pay CDC buyers the outstanding amount of a bond that has defaulted in exchange for premiums paid (typically monthly) by CDC purchasers.

In stable economic conditions, when they work as designed, CDCs enable investors to lend money to some relatively risky ventures (e.g., small high-tech startup businesses) that they might otherwise shun. Ideally, such investments will encourage innovation and creativity by private entrepreneurs while providing a steady, low-risk payment stream to the sellers of CDCs. At the same time, however, as the financial crisis of 2008 illustrates, where many sellers of CDCs are undercapitalized and thus hold only a small percentage of the liquid assets they need to pay for insurance to cover widespread bond defaults, the results can be disastrous.

In mid-2007, the CDC market was at peak levels. At that point, more than $45 trillion had been invested in CDCs—a sum that exceeded the total amount of funds invested in the U.S. stock market, mortgages, and U.S. Treasury bonds combined! Municipal bond purchasers who held CDCs—operating with a false sense of security—bought more and more highly risky debt instruments, including low-rated "junk bonds" and complex derivative instruments that mixed safe assets with risky assets of questionable sustainable value.

In 2008, the credit default market collapsed. An important triggering event in that collapse was the sudden, widely unanticipated collapse of the sprawling Lehman Brothers Investment Bank. This financial giant owed $600 million in bonded debt. Two-thirds of Lehman's debt was covered by CDCs, many of which had been sold to Lehman's bondholders by another very large firm, American Investment Group (AIG). Caught by surprise when Lehman rapidly folded, AIG did not have enough money on hand to cover its swap contracts. Thus, AIG itself teetered on the edge of bankruptcy before its debts were assumed by the Federal Reserve Bank in what came to be called a "bailout."

As they came to realize that CDCs could not cover large, widespread bond defaults, potential purchasers of CDCs declined to buy more of them; and they drastically curtailed their investment practices. At the same time, banks responded to the crisis by becoming more risk averse in their lending practices.

Those adjustments substantially cut off the flow of funds to small businesses and prospective purchasers of private homes. Stock prices collapsed, as did the housing market, and the general economy of the United States and numerous other nations entered into a severe downturn, known as the Great Recession, from which it took many years to recover.

Notes

1. The principal source for the information contained in this section/chapter is Richard J. Miller, *Traditional Bonds and Notes*, *in* State and Local Government Debt Financing (M. David Gelfand ed., Thomson West 2d ed. with supps. 1984) [hereinafter Miller, Chapter 2]. This chapter also draws upon Richard J. Miller, *Creative State and Local Financing Techniques*, and M. David Gelfand, *Taxes and Other Revenue Sources Standing Behind Bonds and Notes*, both in State and Local Government Debt Financing (chs. 4, 10) [hereinafter Miller, Chapter 4, and Gelfand, Chapter 10, respectively]; Robert S. Amdursky & Clayton P. Gillette, Municipal Debt Finance Law (1992); M. David Gelfand et al., State and Local Taxation and Finance in a Nutshell (3d ed. 2007); and various online sources cited below.
2. McQuillin's Law of Municipal Corporations § 43.01 (3d ed. 2018).
3. *See, e.g.*, Tenn. Code Ann. § 67-3-617 (2019); Fla. Stat. § 125.0104(3)(1) (2018).
4. *See* McQuillin's Law of Municipal Corporations, *supra* note 2, § 41.02.
5. *See* Miller, Chapter 2, *supra* note 1, §§ 2:04 and 2:12.
6. *See generally id.* § 2:13.
7. *Id.* § 2:15.
8. *Id.*
9. *Id.*
10. *See id.* § 2:07.
11. *Id.*
12. *See generally id.* § 2:09.
13. *See, e.g.*, N.J. Rev. Stat. § 31:17-46 (2018).
14. *See* Miller, Chapter 2, *supra* note 1, § 2:05.
15. *Id.*
16. *See* Internal Revenue Code §§ 141(d) and 144(c) (1986).
17. *See generally* Gelfand, Chapter 10, *supra* note 1, § 10:20; Miller, Chapter 2, *supra* note 1, § 2:22.
18. *See generally* Gelfand, Chapter 10, *supra* note 1, § 10:20; Miller, Chapter 2, *supra* note 1, § 2:22.
19. Miller, Chapter 4, *supra* note 1, § 2:39.
20. *Id.* § 4:23.

21. *See* Gelfand, Chapter 10, *supra* note 1, § 10:21; Miller, Chapter 2, *supra* note 1, §§ 2:25 to 2:28.
22. Gelfand, Chapter 10, *supra* note 1, § 10:21.
23. *See* Miller, Chapter 2, *supra* note 1, § 2:28.
24. *See* GELFAND ET AL., *supra* note 1, at 215–17.
25. *See generally* Miller, Chapter 4, *supra* note 1, §§ 4:25.21 to 4:25.25.
26. *See* Miller, Chapter 2, *supra* note 1, § 2:32.
27. See *id.* §§ 2:33 to 2:42, and Miller, Chapter 4, *supra* note 1, for more detailed discussions of each of these various types of creative financing.
28. *See* Miller, Chapter 2, *supra* note 1, § 2:32.
29. *Id.* § 2:33.
30. *Id.* § 2:35.
31. *Id.* § 2:36.
32. *Id.*
33. *Id.* § 2:37; Miller, Chapter 4, *supra* note 1, § 4:17.
34. Miller, Chapter 2, *supra* note 1, § 2:38.
35. *Id.* § 2:40.
36. *Id.* § 2:42.
37. *Id.*
38. For a further explanation of catastrophe bonds, see Investopedia, *Catastrophe Bond—CAT*, https://www.investopedia.com/terms/c/catastrophebond.asp (last updated Apr. 25, 2019).
39. *Id.*
40. For an interesting discussion of the advantages of disaster bonds as investment vehicles and as aids to local disaster recovery, see Robert Puentes & Patrick Sabol, *Sandy Recovery: The Case for Disaster Bonds*, BROOKINGS, Dec. 10, 2012, https://www.brookings.edu/blog/the-average/2012/12/10/sandy-recovery-the-case-for-disaster-bonds.
41. A detailed description of this innovative financing instrument can be found at RE.BOUND PROGRAM, LEVERAGING CATASTROPHE BONDS AS A MECHANISM FOR RESILIENT INFRASTRUCTURE PROJECT FINANCE (2015), *available at* http://www.refocuspartners.com/wp-content/uploads/2017/02/RE.bound-Program-Report-December-2015.pdf. *See also* Shalini Vajjhala, *Financing Infrastructure through Resilience Bonds*, BROOKINGS, Dec. 16, 2015, https://www.brookings.edu/blog/the-avenue/2015/12/16/financing-infrastructure-through-resilience-bonds.
42. RE.BOUND PROGRAM, *supra* note 41.
43. The following discussion of credit default swaps is substantially drawn from the cogent analysis presented in Kimberly Amadeo, *Credit Default Swaps with Their Pros, Cons, and Examples*, BALANCE, Dec. 27, 2018, https://www.thebalance.com/credit-default-swaps-pros-cons-crises-examples-3305920.

3

Key Players in the Issuance of Municipal Bonds

A decision to borrow money by issuing public debt is a significant and serious action for elected officials. The statement it makes to voters, investors, and the general public has important consequences and, potentially, a vast impact on future community options. The need for the proposed project that may be financed through borrowing should thus be carefully examined and evaluated. Elected public officials will need to make independent decisions as to what is best for their community. They will be called upon to exercise sound business judgment and to act as a fiduciary of their community's assets. Moreover, once a decision to issue public debt is made, professional advice will be required to assure the success of the transaction.

This chapter identifies the parties and institutions that play a key role in the process of issuing municipal bonds. It also describes the respective roles of those actors in this intricate, and sometimes complicated, process. In determining whether certain municipal needs can best be met by using some form of municipal financing, a community's leaders must take a number of factors into consideration. These include the government's existing resources, any intergovernmental limitations or restrictions on borrowing, the community's income per capita, and community property valuations. The community also must be sensitive to the revenue that it can generate through taxation, any budget deficits that exist, the degree of community dependency on revenue sources, the community's per capita expenditures, the community's general economic health, and its current long-term debt structure. Other factors to be taken into account are the size of the community, the personal income level of the community, and any potential that may exist for overlapping debt obligations. Unfunded liabilities must also be considered, particularly those that relate to future pensions, deferred maintenance, and any other obligations that may not be reflected in the community's budget.

Elected Officials and Appointed Staff Members

Officials and appointed staff are the most important and visible participants in the issuance of public debt. Elected officials will be involved through the entire process, from the decision to use public financing to the ultimate sale and settlement of the bond issue, and it is important that they learn as much as possible about the basic bond transaction. These elected officials will be the ultimate decision makers regarding the appropriateness of public debt, the amount of public debt to be undertaken, and the impact of the public debt on the community and its resources. They must proceed cautiously and prudently, limiting the amount borrowed as much as possible and making certain that the community can meet the terms and conditions of any financial obligations it incurs with as little adverse impact on the community as possible. Elected officials must provide critical information to other participants who assist in the creation, sale, and distribution of the debt. They will also be the voice of the community throughout the process and a source of accurate information for residents and voters with respect to the bond transaction.

As discussed further in Chapter 5, a decision to borrow money through the use of bonds often requires a voter referendum. Therefore, elected public officials must be sensitive to shifting public attitudes and opinions. They must consider the constitution, state law, or home rule charter requirements relating to debt limitations and voter approval, as well as the abilities and skills of the community's own administrators and financial advisors. They must also be sensitive to the risks involved in issuing public debt, the limitations that such debt may place on the community for future generations, and the immediacy of the credit rating impact of the debt on the community's financial standing.

Once there has been an affirmative decision by the public officials (and if necessary by a majority of the citizens) approving the use of public financing, the community's elected officials, its senior management, its chief financial officer, and its legal counsel must determine the workload relating to the project, and they must allocate responsibilities among themselves and outside municipal bond professionals. As noted above, the elected officials are responsible for making policy choices regarding the issuance of public debt or bonds. The chief financial officer is charged with providing all financial and budgetary records to justify and support the public decision to acquire public debt. Additionally—in contrast with attorneys who represent bond industry underwriters and other specialists who have expertise on the economic, financial, and legal requirements that may affect the marketability of the bonds to be issued by the local community—municipal legal counsel must represent the legal interests of the local community.

Financial Advisors

Public financing requires communities to work with a number of participants in the municipal bond industry. Generally, public bodies must seek a financial advisor to advise the governmental unit on the sale of the bonds, the method of financing, and the authorization necessary to complete the issuing process. Usually that advisor will analyze the financial needs of the community and will assist in constructing a bond issue that will carry out the will of the community.[1] Financial advisors typically examine the range of interest payments and other obligations that must be included in the public debt. They also address the status of the bonds under state and federal tax laws and the treatment of various interest payment options. Financial advisors usually examine whether or not issued bonds will be a "qualified tax exempt obligation" and therefore allowable as deductions under the Internal Revenue Code. In fact, some of the work financial advisors will undertake will overlap the efforts of the chief financial officer of the governmental unit and of the underwriter who engages in the sale and distribution of the public debt.

The financial advisor works specifically for the bond issuer, and his or her fees are based on services provided. These fees are separate and distinct from the commissions and fees attached to the transaction by the underwriter and other participants in the issuing process.

The financial advisor generally develops a financing plan to assist the governmental body through the bonding process and makes recommendations regarding how the debt will be structured, the method of sale, and (to some degree) the marketing of the debt. Financial advisors also work closely with modern rating agencies (whose responsibilities are discussed in Chapter 4), and in many cases they will make the final award of sale as a representative of the issuer. The financial advisor participates in the settlement process and in creating a bond record, which is essential for the transaction to be completed. In addition, an independent financial advisor tends to add political credibility to a bond proposal, credibility that can be of considerable help to elected officials where voter approval is required.

Bond Counsel

Communities seeking to issue bonds also generally contract with an outside bond counsel/bond attorney, whose responsibilities include reviewing legal transcripts, approving bond documents required in the jurisdiction, and reviewing the tax-exempt status of the community and its bonds.[2] The bond counsel must determine whether the bond is legal and valid and has the appropriate binding obligations of the issuer.

A bond counsel opinion is of considerable importance. It authorizes the issuance of the security and describes the various procedural steps that must be taken to assure regulatory compliance and federal tax approval. Bond counsel opinions provide an authoritative transcript of the bond proceedings and set forth the bond payment schedule and security arrangements.[3] It is important that the bond counsel be experienced and expert in the interpretation of federal, state, and home rule charter provisions. His or her opinion is relied on by attorneys representing other participants. Although they are reviewed by other attorneys, many of the documents in a bond counsel opinion are the formal documents of the transaction. Bond counsel may also need to determine if any pending litigation might affect the validity of the offering. Occasionally, the bond counsel may seek advice from other bond attorneys if the issuance is a particularly complex transaction or if additional assistance is needed in developing transcripts and the final record.

Underwriters

After a financial advisor and an outside bond counsel have been selected, the next step for a community is to find an appropriate underwriter to arrange financing for the proposed bonds.[4] Underwriters are concerned with originating, structuring, and pricing new municipal bond issues that are sold through a negotiation or bidding process. Specifically, as to those sorts of bonds, an underwriting firm will have responsibility for the following tasks:

1. Assisting in the development of an appropriate credit structure for the bond issue
2. Assisting in the development of the documentation embodying that structure
3. Performing the quantitative analysis necessary to support and justify the structure
4. Creating the maturity structure, pre-redemption or "call" features, and other technical aspects of the bonds
5. Participating in presentations to bond rating agencies
6. Developing and executing comprehensive marketing plans for the bonds
7. Developing and justifying the final pricing for the issue
8. Underwriting the issue, including any balances that remain unsold at the end of the marketing process
9. Assisting in all of the technical aspects of closing the bond sale[5]

It is important to remember that underwriters act as principals. They are not agents of the issuer, and the underwriter is not in a traditional fiduciary relationship with the issuer. Underwriters represent themselves and their clients—clients who are interested in a return on their own investments. Because of the underwriter's independent and self-interested role in the issuance of bonds, bond-issuing communities require the advice and counsel of their own financial and legal advisors.

The role of the underwriter is quite complex. Underwriters provide a significant service to the issuer by attracting investors who will benefit from the specifics of the offering, not the least of which is its tax-exempt yield. Both private investors and institutional buyers influence the bond market, and underwriters must be sensitive to these participants when the offering is structured. In performing their bond structuring function, they must consider bond maturities, repayment schedules, discounts, sinking fund requirements, and rates of interest. Other considerations might include call provisions and the need for insurance guarantees.

A bond underwriter is also responsible for establishing settlement dates, overseeing the printing of the bonds, authentication of fiscal aspects, and delivery of the bonds to the investors or their representatives. Depending upon the size of issue, the type of issue offered, and the complexity of the transaction, additional requirements such as feasibility studies and certifications by certified public accountants may be needed, and frequently the underwriter is responsible for these tasks.[6]

Once the sale is completed, the issuer is responsible for managing the outstanding debt. Usually this is done by a representative of the issuer who acts as a paying agent/registrar, custodian, or trustee. This representative oversees the ongoing requirements related to the specific debt instrument. The issuer itself, however, is responsible for compliance with ongoing regulatory and contractual obligations, and it must adjust its actions as needed to guarantee the eventual success of the bond-financed project.

An underwriter may be part of a major stock brokerage firm, a specialty municipal bond firm, or a commercial bank. Regardless of the form of their businesses, however, underwriters all function in a similar manner. With the help of their counsel (whose responsibilities are described below), underwriters must be capable of navigating state and federal securities laws and other applicable regulations. In addition, after their initial distribution of debt instruments, underwriters are usually responsible for developing and maintaining secondary markets so that bond issues will have adequate liquidity during the life of the obligation.

A typical municipal bond department in an underwriting institution includes trading, sale, research, finance, operations, and underwriting sections. The trading division is maintained for the secondary market for municipal securities and for buying and selling current bonds to investors or other dealers. As noted above, when a bond transaction involves an initial offering, the dealer or underwriter is involved with pricing and distributing the new securities in the primary marketplace.[7] The sales section of the bond department is responsible for making contacts with investors, arranging sales of new or existing securities, and acting as liaison to the trading desk and the underwriting sections of the firm. The bond department also provides municipal research for local government units and suggests alternatives to funding community needs. In addition, the research department may provide short opinions about potential issues and the likelihood of placing such issues. Usually the firm will assign several individuals to develop new products and perform financial advisory work for municipal entities. The operations work in the securities firm deals with the processing of orders and payments, checking and delivering securities, and maintaining customer accounts and government regulatory documentation.

The underwriter stands at the intersection between the supply and demand for capital, and ensures, to the best of its ability, that the transaction will proceed in a timely and orderly way.[8] Through its sales department, the underwriter will participate in conference calls involving the issuer's investment advisor, investment bankers, bond counsel, and representatives of the governmental body. Because of its experience and expertise, the underwriter is typically able to provide current information regarding marketability and activity of investors to the issuer and other participants. The underwriter attempts to price the issue in such a way that it will "clear" the proposed offering and provide the government entity with the funds required. In order to accomplish this, the underwriter must allocate the offering throughout the market in a fair and reasonable manner. This requires that the underwriter understand the needs of the investors, be sensitive to market conditions, and be able to negotiate a price that will be acceptable to both the investor and the issuer.

In order for underwriters to dispose of the issuer's debt obligations, there must be investors who can take advantage of certain tax exemptions, and who are seeking investments that are secure and reliable. Municipal bond investors are often commercial banks, brokerage houses, insurance companies, mutual funds, and occasionally select individuals. The underwriter through its trading department usually seeks groups of investors who can participate in the purchase of the initial offerings, and who are seeking rates, terms, and maturities that match those included in the bond offering. Such a group of investors is typically referred to as a "syndicate" and each participant is a "member of the syndicate."[9]

A syndicate may be of any size, from two investors to more than 100. When groups are large, it is common to appoint a syndicate manager who is responsible for the preparation and submission of the bid to the underwriter.[10] At times, the syndicate manager will also manage the distribution of bonds to members and negotiate the ultimate price for the offering. The exact role of the manager may vary depending on whether the actual offering is sold through a negotiated process or by competitive bidding. Underwriters sometimes participate in "competitive sales" that involve a bidding process between competing syndicates that find the underwriter's offerings attractive. Usually these syndicates will attempt to bargain with the underwriter, and it is the underwriter's responsibility to obtain the highest bid for the issuer. An underwriter may also be involved in "negotiated sales" where the final price for the security is settled through a negotiation process among only a handful of interested buyers. Negotiated sales have grown more popular in recent years. Where an underwriter is having difficulty marketing a particular bond issue, it often retains a bond broker, who is paid a commission to expand the potential market of buyers. The use of a bond broker may reduce the downside risk of the sale, and the broker's special knowledge may help inform the underwriter of possible problems or barriers to the distribution of the obligation.[11]

In sum, the underwriter is one of the most important participants in the issuance of public bonds. The underwriter provides an efficient market for both bond buyers and sellers. Even though underwriters have a clear self-interest with respect to proposed bond issues, their services are essential to communities that wish to market their bonds.

In order to protect their own interests, underwriters usually engage separate legal counsel. In some respects the work of these attorneys is similar to that of bond counsel, and their responsibilities may overlap. In general, an underwriter's counsel assumes the following responsibilities: (1) assisting in structuring the financing and assuring compliance with applicable securities laws (see Chapter 6); (2) conducting "due diligence" inquiries; (3) drafting various documents, including an offering document, a bond purchase agreement, and any needed continuing disclosure agreements, remarketing agreements, and agreements among underwriters; (4) reviewing and commenting on bond documents prepared by other attorneys; (5) preparing any needed blue sky law surveys; and (6) providing opinions on the disclosure of pertinent information and other matters. The first of the tasks is the counsel for the underwriter's most essential task.

In order to prepare the documents necessary for the underwriting of a bond issue, an underwriter's counsel must be involved in early discussions with respect to bond structuring. Such early involvement is necessary in order to provide underwriter's counsel with adequate knowledge of the transaction's purpose and financial strategy so that he or she may knowledgeably integrate the regulatory and tax consequences of the deal into the documents and advice that he or she will prepare.

Early involvement by counsel for the underwriter is also a first step in providing the due diligence required under federal securities laws. Due diligence is likely to include interviews, surveys, written answers to extensive lists of questions, and detailed examinations of compliance with relevant regulations and contracts, tax returns, and management issues. If carried out properly, these inquiries will result in accurate, well-drafted transaction documents, as well as a due diligence defense for the underwriter where questions of liability subsequently arise.

Other Parties

Several other participants are also essential to the issuing of municipal debt. Rating agencies rank initial offerings of municipal bonds as to their creditworthiness. As discussed more fully in Chapter 4, rating agencies play a vital role in ranking the initial creditworthiness of municipal bonds.

Bond insurers also often play a major role. Generally, securities are all subject to some degree of risk, and there is no absolute guarantee as to the safety of any municipal offering. It is possible, however, to reduce the extent of the risk and the possibility of default through the use of insurance, paid for by the bond issuer, that guarantees the payment of principal and interest. Bond insurance, the use of which has grown rapidly in recent years, generally improves the rating of an issue. At the same time, however, such insurance may involve security liens on municipal property as a means of insuring the payment of premiums.

Finally, it should be noted that several other, less visible, parties are also involved in bond transactions. These include paying agents, who receive funds and make payments to bondholders; trustees, who have a fiduciary relationship to bondholders; and depositories, which provide bookkeeping and settlement services for both bond issuers and bondholders.

Notes

1. Financial advisors are persons or firms that represent municipalities in planning, authorization, and sale of bonds to finance public undertakings. Robert L. Ehlers, Ehlers on Public Finance 362 (1998). Typical advisory services provided in connection with a bond issuance include (1) evaluation of an issuer's outstanding debt and borrowing needs; (2) preparation of a request for proposal (RFP) to solicit underwriter suggestions and ideas; (3) evaluation of proposals, whether unsolicited or prepared in response to an RFP; (4) advice on rating agency interactions, or assistance with the development and maintenance of issuer relationships with major rating agencies; (5) development and maintenance of issuer relationships with major bond insurers; (6) scheduling of investor meetings and information calls prior to bond pricing; (7) development of a formal offering memorandum (official statement); (8) review and modifications to key legal documents (e.g., supplemental bond indenture); (9) independent mathematical analysis of financing alternatives under consideration; (10) development of bidding documents and procedures (competitive); (11) allocation of bonds; and (12) review of all aspects of bond pricing (negotiated). Sylvan G. Feldstein & Frank J. Fabozzi, The Handbook of Municipal Bonds 47 (2008).
2. Feldstein & Fabozzi, *supra* note 1, at 69–77.
3. *Id.* at 72–74.
4. *See generally id.* at 25–41; Ehlers, *supra* note 1, at 69–80; Public Securities Association, Fundamentals of Municipal Bonds 69–80 (3d ed. 1987); Moody's Investors Services, Moody's on Municipals 40–45 (1987).
5. Feldstein & Fabozzi, *supra* note 1, at 26.
6. *Id.* at 271.
7. *Id.* at 273–81.
8. *Id.*
9. Public Securities Association, *supra* note 4, at 72.
10. *Id.*
11. Feldstein & Fabozzi, *supra* note 1, at 280–81.

4

The Crucial Role of Rating Agencies

An essential aspect of bond sales is the assignment to a bond issuer of a favorable bond rating by one of the several recognized rating agencies: Moody's Investors Service, Standard & Poor's (S&P), or Fitch Ratings.[1] A favorable rating usually encourages investors to purchase the public offering, it enhances the credibility of the issuer, and it directly affects the prices the bonds will sell for. Only modest differences in bond ratings may have significant impacts on the amount of interest that issuers will be required to pay to bondholders. An agency's rating may also have a significant impact on a community's ability to obtain insurance for its bond instruments. In some cases, however—usually in situations where a proposed bond issue is of a relatively small denomination, or where the issuer is willing to pay a higher interest rate of return than could be obtained if the offering were to have an investment grade attached to it—a bond may be unrated.

Bond ratings have historically provided professional assessments of an issuer's ability to meet its bond obligations, including the likelihood of a bond default and/or tardiness in the payment of bond principal and interest.[2] They are intended to provide investors with reliable information that those investors may draw upon when making their investment decisions. Positive or high bond ratings tend to reflect the general creditworthiness of a community or governmental institution. These ratings provide a quick indication of a far more detailed analysis of public and nonpublic information that, when taken together, typically yields an accurate judgment regarding the safety and security of a specific public security. In fact, bond ratings alone may determine the relative success or failure of a given offering.[3]

In the United States, rating systems or agencies are approximately 100 years old.[4] Two of the largest agencies, Moody's and S&P, emerged as a result of public involvement in a variety of financial problems caused by failed land schemes and the unsuccessful funding of new railroad ventures. From the late 1800s and early 1900s to World War I there was a rapid expansion of investment information services, of which Moody's and S&P were the early leaders.[5]

Following the 2008 financial crisis, rating agencies were sharply criticized for failing to adequately report the changing creditworthiness of certain public debt instruments. They were also accused of having conflicts of interest and providing inflated bond ratings. These criticisms led to something of a decline in public confidence in the agencies; and to some extent large municipal investors relied for a time on their own due diligence investigations—instead of rating agencies—to protect their financial interests. However, to a significant extent, rating agencies have restored investor confidence in their assessments of municipal bond offerings.

Changing economic conditions and tax laws have had an important influence on the sale of municipal or government bonds. As discussed further in Chapter 6, in the late 20th century, two public financing failures were especially well publicized: the default of notes issued by New York City in 1975 and the Washington Public Power Supply System revenue bonds default in 1983. A significant factor in the development of the municipal and government bond market was the creation of the Municipal Securities Rulemaking Board (MSRB) in 1975 that began to regulate brokers and dealers in the municipal securities industry.[6] Finally, the advent of junk bonds in the 1980s generated further interest by investors in sound, objective bond-related analysis and evaluation.

Criticism Following the 2008 Financial Crisis

As noted above, after the financial crisis of 2008, rating agencies suffered from a loss of credibility. They came under mounting pressure from the U.S. Securities and Exchange Commission (SEC), investors, municipalities, and the public regarding their role in the global credit collapse. Christopher Cox, former chair of the SEC, indicated that a commission he headed had uncovered serious shortcomings with the rating agencies, including a failure to disclose information to investors, a lack of appropriate policies and procedures, and inattention to conflicts of interest.[7] Moody's, S&P, and Fitch were all criticized for not acknowledging emerging financial problems in many companies, thereby appearing to give continued approval to bonds they had previously rated. According to the Cox Commission report,[8] when the rating bodies did react it was too late.

Their failure to react quickly, clearly, and with some degree of transparency also had a negative impact on municipal and government bond issues, even though these public bonds have had many fewer defaults than corporate bonds, and investors in them have seldom lost money.[9]

Credit Rating Agency Reform Act

Shortly before the credit meltdown of 2008, President Bush signed into law the Credit Rating Agency Reform Act, a statute designed to correct some of the prior problems and abuses.[10] The regulatory response was to create a "nationally recognized statistical rating organization" (NRSRO) that addressed some of the conflict-of-interest problems and some questions of transparency. In addition, the law proposed regulations that would create criteria for defining and designating NRSROs.[11] This law established procedures for becoming a qualified rating agency that included descriptions of the firm's experience, the extent of its contacts with bond issuers, the organizational structure of the rating agency, its financial conditions and resources, the number of issues it manages, and its methods of monitoring and enforcing compliance procedures.[12] In addition, the act required the disclosure of the rating agency's information sources and how that information is utilized.

In recent years, three other factors have also had a significant impact on the bond rating business: globalization or internationalization of the capital markets, increased competition, and innovation in financial instruments.[13] The internationalization factor reflects the increased demand and need for the rating of bonds, both commercial and public, for the European and Asian markets. Foreign competitors and new national niche specialists, who may provide more customized services and/or lower fees, have emerged; and there has been an increase in various innovative derivatives and structured financings that require agencies to perform new forms of analysis in shorter time frames. Each of these changes seems to have influenced bond rating agencies in the direction of relaxing their traditional standards and revising their standard procedures.

Influence of Rating Agencies

Notwithstanding their shortcomings and difficulties, bond rating agencies can have immense influence on the fiscal and budgetary policies of local governments. One example of that influence may be seen in the actions of the city of Philadelphia, which experienced declining bond ratings, and an inability to raise cash, during the 1990s. In an effort to find needed funds and prevent insolvency, Philadelphia, on the recommendation of its bond rater, changed the investment policies that guided its union pension account. Moreover, after the election of a new mayor who wished to improve the city's bond rating, Philadelphia instituted draconian budget restrictions that eventually satisfied its bond rating agency. The city's bonds were ultimately upgraded as a result.

Another illustration of the potential power of bond rating agencies with regard to municipal fiscal policies can be seen in the city of Detroit. Like Philadelphia, for a number of years Detroit had faced economic decline, increasing unemployment, decreased per capita income, and a loss of population. As a result of these conditions, Detroit's bond ratings had been lowered to a low investment grade level, requiring the city to offer higher interest rates to attract bond purchasers. When a new mayor was elected, he responded positively and aggressively to rating agency suggestions for budget cuts. As a direct result, the rating agencies upgraded the city's bond ratings five times.

Credibility of Rating Agencies

As noted above, the credibility of rating agencies lies in the validity of their assessments, the objectivity of their analyses, and the reliance investors and issuers place on their recommendations/ratings. Bond issuers and investors need to understand the various rating systems used by the individual rating agencies, and what each rating signals regarding the risk involved in the specific issues. They must be aware that ratings refer only to specific instruments. Those ratings make no judgment about the institution issuing the instrument, nor do ratings generate any fiduciary relationship between the rating agency and the investor. At the same time, however, because of the reliance that the investment community has traditionally placed in bond rating agencies, those agencies need to be sensitive to the potential consequences of any failures on their part to notify investors, in a timely manner, of factors that may affect the accuracy of existing bond ratings. Moreover, bond issuers and investors should be made aware of any potential conflicts of interest that may affect the objectivity of bond raters and their work products.

Typically, rating agencies are paid for their work by bond issuers. Investors frequently question this system of payment for services as having the potential to impair the impartiality of bond raters. The objectivity of rating agencies was also called into question recently when it was discovered that rating agencies provided drafts of proposed rating reports to bond issuers before those reports were finally released. Obviously, such exchanges raise questions as to how much influence an issuer may have upon the rater to reframe, restate, or change unfavorable information.[14]

Another troubling rating agency practice, which investors sometimes question, is that of providing private credit opinions to bond issuers before their rating evaluations begin. Even though those private agency opinions do not provide an exact bond issue rating, they do provide the issuers with a broad summary indicating the type of rating that might be given to their instruments. This arrangement provides issuers with a market advantage that some perceive as improper.

Should a Rating Be Sought?

Before contacting a bond rating agency, bond issuers must decide whether they wish to proceed with a bond rating application. Some issuers may be able to find private investors who are willing to negotiate terms regarding the proposed bond issue. If an issuer can reach an agreement with those investors, there may be no need for a rating decision. At the same time, however, an issuer that privately sells an unrated instrument will run a risk that prior ratings that have been assigned to similar securities it has issued publicly will be withdrawn.

Before deciding whether to apply for a bond rating, issuers must also consider the cost and inconvenience of doing so. Rating agency fees are not insubstantial. Depending on the amount of the issue, agency fee totals may exceed $100,000—including such items as the cost of compiling and maintaining numerous documents, financial advisory fees that are separate from rating fees, and the costs of all monitoring and compliance assessments that will occur once a rating decision has been made. Moreover, even though issuers may ask rating agencies to delay their ratings decisions for limited periods of time, their long-term borrowing prospects and financial reputations may well suffer if they attempt to withdraw from an ongoing ratings exercise out of a concern that it will result in a lower bond rating than they anticipated initially.

The Rating Process

Application Review and Decision

Once a local government decides to seek a bond agency rating, the rating process begins. A representative of the issuer—usually a city manager, administrator, chief financial officer, or financial advisor—will notify the rating agency and formally request a rating. Following this, the issuer will complete various application forms prescribed by the agency and submit numerous other documents. The rating agency's staff will then begin to review and evaluate the data submitted to them and identify other formal and informal sources of pertinent information.

After some preliminary research has been conducted by the agency—and after any necessary meetings (including onsite visits) to resolve unanswered agency staff questions and concerns—the agency will make a tentative conclusion available to the issuer. After any further needed consultations between the agency and the issuer have taken place, and any lingering questions have been resolved to the extent possible, the agency's rating committee will present a recommendation to the issuer. After that has occurred (assuming no appeal is taken by the issuer), the agency will provide the issuer and the public with a formal notification of the bond issue's rating. Once the rating has been issued, the agency will continue to monitor the financial condition and activities of the issuer.

Appeal from Ratings Decisions

It is possible for issuers to appeal an agency's rating decision by formally requesting reconsideration and submitting additional or updated data. Where such a request raises questions that were not previously considered by the agency and might warrant reconsideration, the agency may be willing to undertake an additional evaluation. If so, the agency's bond rating committee will discuss the matter again and determine whether to confirm or modify its previous determination. Where an appeal is granted and pressed, representatives of the issuer would do well to make a personal visit to the rating agency, and to provide as much new data as possible regarding changed circumstances and improved financial conditions. Such data may make it easier for the rating agency to justify a modification of its previous determination. However, since agencies typically tend to be reluctant to acknowledge that their initial determinations were faulty, ratings appeals by issuers generally do not succeed.

Ratings Definitions

Bond rating agencies vary somewhat in their approaches and in the ways that they define their rating categories. The general categories for agency rating systems include long- and short-term ratings. In addition, some of the agencies provide ratings for commercial paper, short-term notes, and debt and demand obligations.[15] The differences among the three major rating agencies can be seen by comparing how each agency rates long-term municipal bonds, both in relation to each other and with respect to risk and creditworthiness.

Moody's long-term ratings are designed to measure the possibility of loss or "expected loss." They therefore include factors reflecting the probability of a default and the expected severity of a loss should a default occur. The agency renders opinions of the credit quality of specific obligations or general creditworthiness of the issuer. Moody's credit analysis of a governmental body's ability to finance its proposed obligation relies on four primary factors: economic conditions, institutional debt, financial strength or weakness, and administration/management strategies.[16] The Moody's ranking consists of nine grades ranging from Aaa to C, which reflect, from top to bottom, instruments that range from very high investment grades to highly speculative or noninvestment grades.[17] Moody's uses numerical modifiers to indicate whether the issue is at the top or in the middle or bottom of a particular rating.[18] Moody's also uses conditional ratings to highlight specific circumstances.

S&P uses a similar but slightly modified ranking system. S&P ranks issues from AAA to D SD. Like Moody's ratings, S&P's ratings range from highest-grade ratings to obligations in default.[19] S&P uses plus+ or minus– modifiers to indicate the relative strength or weakness of an issue within a given ranking.[20]

Fitch rates its issues like the others by a schedule ranging from AAA to D. AAA indicates the strongest investment grade. Obligations in default are assigned a D rating.[21] Fitch ratings are a benchmark to suggest the likelihood of default by the issuer in meeting its payment obligation.[22] The investment grade ratings of Moody's, S&P, and Fitch are illustrated in the following table.

Basic Long-Term Rating Comparisons

Moody's	S&P	Fitch
Aaa	AAA	AAA
Aa	AA	AA
A	A	A
Baa	BBB	BBB
Ba	BB	BB
B	B	B
Caa	CCC	CCC
Ca	CC	CC
C	C	C
	D SD	D
		NR

For an explanation of the ratings definitions used by these three major bond rating agencies, see the appendix to this chapter.

Although, as discussed above, each bond rating agency has its own unique system, certain factors usually are present in each rating scheme. Economic conditions are the most difficult of those factors to measure and evaluate. Every community is influenced by the regional and national economy, but communities cannot generally control the impact of such economic conditions as employment levels, demographics trends, trade balances, inflation, and business cycles. These factors nonetheless play a significant role in a community's ability to meet its financial obligations. General and specific economic data such as local unemployment numbers and trends, the quality, type, and success of local businesses, and long-term regional and national trends can be accurate measures of a local government's ability to issue and meet new financial commitments. Other factors that are important in rating decisions are the general wealth of the community, its tax base, and its past record of principal and interest payments on general obligation and revenue bonds. The levels of a community's retail sales, building permits issued, and any pending lawsuits or legal claims against the community may also be relevant factors in rating decisions.

The debt factor of a community is especially important to rating agencies. The amount of debt held by a community relative to its taxable property, the community's total amount of debt, its current debt repayments schedule, future expectations of new debt, and its types and varieties of credit instruments may all directly influence the eventual rating of an issue. Another important factor may be the amount of debt held by adjacent or overlapping political jurisdictions, since local property tax revenues may be used for a number of geographically related obligations.

All rating agencies tend to examine the following indicators of a community's financial health: financial statements, schedules of revenue sources, capital and general operating budgets along with actual performance budgets, lists of community assets and liabilities, community projections of future expenditures, specific fund balances, financial policy statements, and contingency plans. Other financial factors that might influence the quality of a particular rating are the extent of a community's compliance with the Government Finance Officers Association's (GFOA's) practices and the guidelines of generally accepted accounting principles (GAAP). Still other items that will be examined in the rating process are independent audit documents, management letters, and selected reports or analyses of revenues, expenditures, and short-term and long-term liabilities. The latter tend to include pension and benefit statements, labor settlements, financial obligations relating to joint-powers agreements, and any other inter-local government commitments.

A final category that rating agencies examine is a community's administrative practices. Relevant areas of inquiry may include the size and quality of the community's professional staff and their line responsibilities, the extent to which its administrative procedures ensure public participation, the community's level of compliance with regulatory standards, and how efficiently it implements community services and meets constituent needs. These factors may be difficult to measure or quantify. Community leaders, both elected and appointed, must understand the role and obligations they owe to the community, and they must have the ability to plan and implement ongoing programs, to adjust and change policies in order to reflect current economic, political, environmental, and social needs, and to make reasonable and timely financial decisions as needed.

Appendix

Ratings Definitions of Major Bond Rating Agencies

Moody's Ratings and Municipal Long-Term Rating Definitions

Rating	Municipal Long-Term Rating Definitions
Aaa	Issuers or issues rated Aaa demonstrate the strongest creditworthiness relative to other U.S. municipal or tax-exempt issuers or issues.
Aa	Issuers or issues rated Aa demonstrate very strong creditworthiness relative to other U.S. municipal or tax-exempt issuers or issues.
A	Issuers or issues rated A demonstrate above-average creditworthiness relative to other U.S. municipal or tax-exempt issuers or issues.
Baa	Issuers or issues rated Baa demonstrate average creditworthiness relative to other U.S. municipal or tax-exempt issuers or issues.
Ba	Issuers or issues rated Ba demonstrate below-average creditworthiness relative to other U.S. municipal or tax-exempt issuers or issues.
B	Issuers or issues rated B demonstrate weak creditworthiness relative to other U.S. municipal or tax-exempt issuers or issues.
Caa	Issuers or issues rated Caa demonstrate very weak creditworthiness relative to other U.S. municipal or tax-exempt issuers or issues.
Ca	Issuers or issues rated Ca demonstrate extremely weak creditworthiness relative to other U.S. municipal or tax-exempt issuers or issues.
C	Issuers or issues rated C demonstrate the weakest creditworthiness relative to other U.S. municipal or tax-exempt issuers or issues.

S&P Ratings and Municipal Issuer/Issue Long-Term Rating Definitions

Rating	Municipal Issuer/Issue Long-Term Rating Definitions
AAA	An obligor/obligation rated AAA has extremely strong capacity to meet its financial commitments.
AA	An obligor/obligation rated AA has very strong capacity to meet its financial commitments, differing from AAA rated issuers/issues only to a small degree.
A	An obligor/obligation rated A has strong capacity to meet its financial commitments.
BBB	An obligor/obligation rated BBB has adequate capacity to meet its financial commitments.
BB	An obligor/obligation rated BB is less vulnerable in the near term than other lower-rated issuers/issues; however, it faces major ongoing uncertainties and exposure to adverse business and economic conditions that could lead to inadequate capacity to meet its financial commitments.
B	An obligor/obligation rated B is more vulnerable to nonpayment than issuers/issues rated higher but has the capacity to meet its financial commitments. Adverse conditions will likely impair the ability to meet the financial commitments.
CCC	An obligor/obligation rated CCC is currently vulnerable to nonpayment and is dependent on favorable business, financial, and economic conditions to meet its financial commitments.
CC	An obligor/obligation rated CC is currently highly vulnerable to nonpayment.
C	An obligation is rated C to cover a situation where a bankruptcy petition has been filed, or similar action has been taken, but payments on this obligation are being continued.

Fitch Ratings and Municipal Long-Term Credit Rating Definitions

Rating	Municipal Long-Term Credit Rating Definitions
AAA	Highest credit quality. AAA ratings denote the lowest expectation of credit risk, assigned only in the case of exceptionally strong capacity for payment of financial commitments.
AA	Very high credit quality. AA ratings denote expectations of very low credit risk and indicate very strong capacity for payment of financial commitments.
A	High credit quality. A ratings denote expectations of low credit risk and indicate strong capacity for payment of financial commitments. This capacity may, nevertheless, be more vulnerable to changes in circumstances or in economic conditions than is the case for higher ratings.
BBB	Good credit quality. Moderate credit risk. BBB ratings indicate that there are currently expectations of low credit risk. The capacity for payment of financial commitments is considered adequate, but adverse changes in circumstances and economic conditions are more likely to impair this capacity.
BB	Speculative. Elevated default risk. BB ratings indicate that there is a possibility of credit risk developing, particularly as the result of adverse economic change over time; however, business or financial alternatives may be available to allow financial commitments to be met.
B	Highly speculative. Significantly elevated default risk. For issuers and performing obligations, B ratings indicate that significant credit risk is present, but a limited margin of safety remains.
CCC	For issuers and performing obligations, CCC ratings indicate that default is a real possibility.
CC	For issuers and performing obligations, CC ratings indicate default of some kind appears probable.
C	For issuers and performing obligations, C ratings indicate default is imminent.
D	D indicates an entity that has defaulted on all of its financial obligations.

Notes

1. Timothy J. Sinclair, The New Masters of Capital: American Bond Rating Agencies and the Politics of Creditworthiness 1 (2005).
2. Sylvan G. Feldstein & Frank J. Fabozzi, The Handbook of Municipal Banks 23 (2008).
3. Robert L. Ehlers, Ehlers on Public Finance 187 (1998).
4. Lawrence J. White, *A New Law for the Bond Rating Industry*, Regulation, Spring 2007, at 48.
5. Sinclair, *supra* note 1, at 25.
6. Public Securities Association, Fundamentals of Municipal Bonds 5 (3d ed. 1987).
7. Paul J. Davies et al., *Reputations to Restore*, Fin. Times, July 21, 2008.
8. *Oversight of Nationally Recognized Statistical Ratings Organizations, Hearing before the U.S. Senate Committee on Banking, Housing, and Urban Affairs*, 110th Cong. (2008) (testimony of SEC Chairman Christopher Cox), https://www.sec.gov/news/testimony/2008/ts042208cc.htm.
9. *Id.*
10. White, *supra* note 4, at 48.
11. *Id.* at 50.
12. *Id.* at 51.
13. Sinclair, *supra* note 1, at 27.
14. David Cay Johnston, *Objectivity of a Rating Questioned*, N.Y. Times, Dec. 12, 2008, at 1.
15. Feldstein & Fabozzi, *supra* note 2, at 224–33.
16. *Id.* at 225.
17. *Id.*
18. *Id.*
19. *Id.* at 227.
20. *Id.*
21. *Id.* at 232.
22. *Id.* at 231.

5

State Law Limitations on Local Government Borrowing

Introduction

Local government borrowing differs in a fundamental way from either individual or corporate debt. Nongovernmental lending concentrates on the creditworthiness and security of the particular borrower. In the event of default in the repayment of interest or principal on this form of borrowing, the financial liability stemming from nonpayment will be focused upon the privately owned assets of the particular borrower. The lender making the loan will initially assess the creditworthiness of the borrower in choosing to extend credit and later will seek payment out of the debtor's assets if sufficient repayment fails. These are the characteristics of a private transaction.

When local governments borrow money for governmental purposes, the borrower is an entity having special characteristics that differ from private actors. The local government exists solely to provide governmental services and not for profit-making reasons. Local governments, while not private corporations, are not exempt from the claims of creditors. In fact, the federal bankruptcy law makes special provision in Chapter 9 for municipal bankruptcies, granting protection for a financially distressed municipality from its creditors while allowing it to develop a plan for adjusting its debts. Bankruptcy law also provides relief for private debtors. However, in comparison to the bankruptcy law for private companies, Chapter 9 contains no provision for the liquidation of governmental assets and the distribution of the proceeds to creditors. This should not be surprising since the local government owns property and provides services exclusively for the public benefit.

Local governments also differ from private, profit-making entities in their ability to raise revenues through a unique means not possessed by private corporations or individuals: they can impose taxes that must be paid by those within its taxing jurisdiction. Since this form of governmental undertaking is often financed using long-term debt that may span several decades, a local government debtor frequently passes its obligations to later residents and taxpayers who did not approve the initial borrowing decision. These citizens can be saddled with long-lasting financial obligations incurred many years earlier, perhaps with few direct benefits to them. This notion of intergenerational cost-shifting is scarcely new. In fact, it prompted James Madison to suggest in a letter that the maximum term for public debt should be constitutionally set at 19 years.[1] In more recent times, this potential transfer of costs to future generations has motivated legislatures to define tight parameters for municipal debt issuance, and it has prompted courts to monitor compliance very closely.

Today, local governments provide a wide range of services to their residents, and their public facilities are often capital-intensive. It is not uncommon for a public high school to cost more than $50 million to construct; and larger public projects, such as those involving transportation, can cost billions of dollars. Due to their limited financial resources, localities are forced to look for external funding to finance these projects. As with the acquisition of most costly assets in American society, states and localities borrow money from the capital markets to finance construction and improvement of most of their infrastructure and other community facilities. These government entities use the relatively low debt service costs available to them to spread out the construction costs of new schools, fire and police stations, libraries, and other facilities over many years.

As discussed further in Chapter 7, state and municipal debt is often attractive to bond buyers because the interest payments they receive may be exempt from federal and/or state income taxation.[2] It should be noted that localities may also issue debt whose interest payments are fully taxable to their owners.[3] For example, municipal bonds with fully taxable interest payments have been issued in nine states in order to help debt-strapped homeowners refinance existing high-interest-rate, adjustable loans into more affordable long-term, fixed-rate mortgages.[4] Notably, municipal interest in preventing residential mortgage foreclosures extends beyond concern about homeowners. Localities also have a systematic interest in preventing mortgage failures since the sharp increase in residential mortgages during the past several years has led capital markets to be much more restrictive in funding all local government debt issues. This has had an adverse effect on municipal financing of many public improvements such as schools, transportation projects, recreation facilities, and airports.[5]

The special power to acquire capital for public benefit through the issuance of public debt instruments has been exercised by states and local governments for nearly as long as our country's history.[6] At times, however, the popular will to improve the local government facilities and services has resulted in an overreliance on borrowed funds exceeding the government's capacity to repay. In fact, excessive borrowing led to serious financial difficulties in the first half of the 19th century when states aggressively sought to encourage economic development through bond-financed construction of major transportation systems such as the Erie Canal.[7] During this early period, a number of states could not service their debts through tax revenues and project receipts, and a number of them defaulted on their debts.[8] In the last quarter of the 19th century, many American cities followed the earlier pattern set by the states. They overborrowed in support of their own entrepreneurial activity, which was usually undertaken for the benefit of private business, and, thereafter, the government entity defaulted on its debt. The financial implications of these irresponsible practices were devastating. Following the Panic of 1873 and the years of economic contraction, municipal bond issuance was greatly reduced.[9] In the wake of this crisis, credit became tight and taxes rose to provide for the necessary debt service.

As a result of massive 19th-century state and local bond defaults, state legislatures demonstrated heightened awareness of the risks associated with the issuance of excessive municipal debt. States began to adopt a number of state debt restrictions to prevent the recurrence of the financially destructive behavior that had coincided with earlier panics and depressions. Most of these protective mechanisms are still in force and can be found in state constitutions and statutes.[10] Some states have adopted legislation that comprehensively seeks to regulate government borrowing and attempts to avoid excessive state and local government debt. Others have taken a narrower, more focused approach. The most common regulatory devices include:

1. Limits on the amount of debt that may be outstanding at any time (debt limits or ceilings)
2. Process requirements for local government debt issuance and voter approval
3. Requirements for the mandatory levy of sufficient annual tax revenues to service outstanding debt
4. Prohibition of the governmental gift or loan of money or credit to persons and private businesses (lending of credit prohibitions)
5. Restrictions on new debt issuances to those that serve a public purpose

All of these mechanisms have been implemented for two general purposes: (1) to protect the state and its citizens from uncontrollable debt, damaged government credit, and resulting high taxes; and (2) to protect bondholders from being left with invalid bonds.

Debt Limitations or Debt Ceilings

All states have adopted some form of debt limitations, and "[t]he vast majority of state constitutions impose some limitation on the ability of their state and local governments to incur debt."[11] Alaska, Connecticut, Mississippi, Nebraska, New Hampshire, Tennessee, and Vermont appear to be exceptions by imposing no limits at either the state or local level. Moreover, bond issues that exceed debt limitations are typically considered *ultra vires* and void. The effectiveness of the "debt ceiling" policy approach has been criticized by some observers.[12] Its continuing justification is that debt limits serve as "a means of reconciling the conflict between short-term and long-term interests that debt generates."[13] In other words, debt ceilings recognize the need for state policies that limit the ability of politicians and residents to finance projects that will burden future generations.

Some state laws target local governments but do not place limitations on state borrowing.[14] These debt restrictions may originate in constitutions, statutes, or charters. When they are found in constitutional provisions they must be observed with considerable fidelity to the constitutional text. However, statewide uniformity is not always required. Several states have vested the power to expand borrowing power in individual instances. For example, Kansas's constitution delegates debt regulation to the legislature, thus requiring the passage of statutes authorizing debt financing.[15] Maryland's constitution forbids counties from lending their credit but allows the legislature to grant them that power subject to certain restrictions.[16] In contrast to constitutional debt limitations, this method is extremely flexible. Under it, the state legislature may exempt a given municipality from debt limitations under certain circumstances, change debt ceilings put in place by prior statutes, or even ratify excess debt by a curative act.[17] The ultimate responsibility in this system rests with the elected state legislature.

Examining all of the states, it is apparent that a wide variety of approaches are taken. The most common form of debt limitation is a restriction on the amount of outstanding debt that a locality may have.[18] However, there seems to be no unifying theory for setting restrictions on the maximum amount of state and local debt. Constitutional and statutory provisions sometimes establish absolute ceilings on debt, forbidding an entity from exceeding a specified amount.[19] For instance, California sets this limit at $300,000[20] while Washington State has established $400,000[21] and Arizona $350,000.[22] These amounts may be exceeded only if the issuing entity invokes an exception listed in the constitution. Occasionally, the maximum debt amount is expressed as a percentage of annual appropriations[23] or a percentage of annual tax or other kinds of revenue.[24]

Alternatively though, and more commonly, these limits impose a debt cap based on a percentage of the assessed or full value of real estate within the jurisdiction, as determined by state or local assessors, appraisers, tax commissioners, or boards of equalization.[25] Once again there appears to be no consistent pattern with respect to limitation amounts. For example, the Iowa Constitution forbids any county or other local government from becoming "indebted in any manner" in an amount exceeding 5 percent per annum of the value of the taxable property within the jurisdiction.[26] In Virginia, the state's constitution sets the figure at 10 percent of assessed valuation,[27] while in Minnesota the legislature has limited cities to a debt up to 2 percent of the market value of all taxable property within the city.[28] In some jurisdictions, the "hard caps" imposed by these debt limitations may be exceeded to a preset amount with voter approval through a bond referendum.[29] And some states set variable percentages based upon the size[30] or type of municipality.[31]

In those states limiting debt to a stated percentage of taxable property, judicial interpretation of the pertinent language of limitation has been especially important. The term "taxable property" has been given a broad reading by reviewing courts. It has been read to include all forms of property—both real and personal—that are subject to taxation. Courts have interpreted the term "assessed value" in state constitutional and statutory provisions in various ways. When the word "value" is not preceded by the word "assessed," a majority of courts have held that it refers to the property's actual value.[32] A minority position taken in some states is that the term "value" standing alone refers to assessed value, or the value upon which taxes are calculated.[33] Generally, however, the full phrase "assessed value" is deemed to refer to the assessed value of property for tax calculation purposes.[34] And in Guam, the U.S. Supreme Court has interpreted the territory's Organic Act (48 U.S.C. § 1423a), which proscribes public indebtedness exceeding 10 percent per year of the "aggregate tax valuation of the property in Guam," as meaning the assessed valuation of that property.[35]

The Avoidance of Debt Limitations

Debt Ceilings and Their Application

Because most constitutional debt limitations are quite restrictive, many exceptions have been developed over the years in order to permit more debt financing for governmental infrastructure development. These exceptions are often openly identified when they are enumerated in a state's constitution. Some jurisdictions, for example, have separate limits or even no limitations on borrowing for public utilities. In New York, for instance, the state's constitution excludes borrowing for water projects from the state debt limitation.[36] A number of other states exempt debt incurred for any form of public works improvement.[37] Many jurisdictions also allow excess debt when it is borrowed in exceptional circumstances including when necessary to suppress insurrection, repel invasion, or support defense.[38] Other states allow debt in excess of the usual limits following man-made or natural disasters.[39]

Some states expressly exclude the "ordinary and necessary" expenses of a governmental unit from debt calculation.[40] This is because "the term 'debt' generally does not encompass current expenses."[41] As such, appropriations made to pay for current governmental expenses are typically not included in calculations of debt limitations.[42] This logic has given rise to a more recently developed form of "nondebt debt" called subject-to-appropriations debt.[43] Although some states expressly exclude "current" expenses from debt calculations in their constitutions,[44] the notion that subject-to-appropriations debt is not really "debt" is mostly a function of judicial interpretation. Other states have judicially interpreted "ordinary and necessary" exceptions in a restrictive fashion.[45] "Necessary" expenses are typically interpreted as those that are involuntarily incurred or that are used to maintain essential functions of the public entity.[46] Obligations imposed on a municipality by a state government, therefore, are not generally considered to be debt.[47] For example, in *Los Angeles County v. Byram*, the Supreme Court of California held that because the county's duty to provide adequate courthouses was legally mandated by the state, the construction of a courthouse was not debt.[48] Necessity is often subject to conservative judicial interpretation, requiring some threat to the existence of the municipality such as a popularly perceived emergency. These emergencies have included payment of police and firefighter salaries, protection of public health, construction of jails, construction of flood walls, and obtaining of voting machines, to name a few.[49] Other judicially excepted forms of debt include tax anticipation notes (TANs), revenue anticipation notes (RANs),[50] bonds issued to refund existing debt,[51] and debts arising from payment of tort judgments.[52]

Special Fund Doctrine

Because, by definition, a debt limitation may not be exceeded, most avoidance techniques consist of financing projects with borrowed money that is not considered to be "debt" in terms of constitutional and statutory debt limitations. One early limitation avoidance method was to exclude bonds that financed revenue-producing projects from the strictures of state debt limitations. The notion behind this view, which became known as the "special fund doctrine," was that the repayment of the project-related debt was secured by revenues generated by the project into a "special fund." General tax receipts and the general credit of the local government were not jeopardized by this method of finance. An example of this kind of financing would be the construction of a municipal parking facility where the debt service would be covered with the parking receipts generated by the building.

Historically, the only revenue bonds exempt from debt limitations were project finance bonds (e.g., bonds issued to finance a project whose revenues would be used to pay off the debt incurred for the project). State courts found that as long as the state limited its debt service payment obligation to the special fund generated by the project, such a revenue bond was not debt subject to the debt limit.[53] Similarly, site-specific improvements such as sidewalks, street repairs or construction, and curbs and gutters, whose capital costs were to be paid exclusively from special assessments charged to adjoining property owners, did not create debt under the legal doctrine prevalent in the United States.[54]

Other Evasions of Debt Limitations

The success of the special fund doctrine in circumventing state limits encouraged local governments to expand the concept. The attractive prospect of finding alternative means of financing a wide range of public improvements and facilities in ways that were not constrained by debt limits challenged the ingenuity of municipal attorneys and bond counsel. Eventually, state courts began to expand the special fund doctrine, finding that a wide array of projects fell outside of the definition of "debt." The Oklahoma Supreme Court, for example, held that bonds issued to finance new highways were not "debt" because the new road would increase automobile usage while being subjected to additional fuel tax and related fees. Similarly, in Hawaii, a convention center financed with public bonds was held not to create debt because a new tax on hotels, coupled with the increased tourism created by the convention center, would create sufficient revenue to pay the debt service.[55]

Other techniques have also been developed to evade state constitutional or statutory debt limitations. These mechanisms include lease financing, special districts and authorities, service contracts[56] and subject-to-appropriations debt, special assessments, tax increment financing, and certificates of participation (COPs).

Leases

Leases are one commonly used method of debt limitation avoidance since they are not considered to be debt if there is no obligation to pay annual obligations in the future.[57] The justification for not treating leases as forms of current debt derives from long-standing ideas regarding the rights that spring from a lease. Under the common law view of the lease, the rent sprang from the leased land and established a recurring obligation at the time it became due under the terms of the lease.[58] Courts would then attempt to distinguish *bona fide* local government leases (which typically involved periodic rental payments, often with an option to purchase at the end of the rental period) from installment contracts (which usually involved periodic payments made to retire an aggregate sum, the full payment of which would result in transfer of title to the public entity).[59] Generally, bona fide leases were not considered to be debt because the only obligation they created was the payment of rent as it became due. Installment purchase contracts, on the other hand, would be considered debt, since they represented a series of payments that implicitly incorporated interest payments, and since they led to the eventual transfer of ownership to the "purchasing" local government.

Some courts have ruled that long-term leases are to be deemed debt for the purposes of computing debt limitations, finding the device to be illusory and to constitute a burden on future taxpayers without voter approval.[60] This is especially likely to be the outcome when courts conclude that the lease arrangement is a bad-faith attempt to mask a conditional sale with installment payments. In such instances, courts tend to consider the total amount to be debt calculable toward the ceiling, and if the ceiling is exceeded the contract will be voided.[61] Factors looked to as evidence of bad-faith concealment of a sale include immediate debt for the aggregate of rentals, and, in particular, options for purchase for little or no additional consideration upon completion of the term of rent. There is a tendency on the part of some courts to hold leases-veiled-as-sales to be debt when the project financed is highly expensive (i.e., a stadium or convention center) or when it is not to be used for ordinary government purposes.[62] Other courts, however, are more deferential toward transactions that are only thinly veiled as leases.[63]

Sale-and-Lease-Back Techniques

A variation on lease financing is the use of sale-and-lease-back provisions. These involve the issuance of bonds by a public authority or even private corporation that then builds and holds the title to a building. The authority or company then leases the building to a state or local government. Private debts clearly are not subject to state or local debt limitations, and it is now close to doctrinal that "debts of public authorities are not debts in the constitutional sense because the authorities lack the capacity to impose taxes or pledge the full faith and credit of the state or local government."[64] The lease payments are used by the bond issuing authority or company to pay the debt service. As such, the rent payments are "not on the market value of the lease but on the private firm's or public authority's debt service requirements."[65] Because the payment of the lease is subject to appropriation by the legislature on a year-by-year basis, and there is no obligation on future legislatures to pay the lease, the payments are generally not found to constitute debt.[66] In most instances, if the legislature were to choose not to appropriate the funds necessary to pay the lease, the building could be leased to another party and the bond issuer could continue to pay debt service on its bonds. This is not the case for certain types of buildings, however, such as prisons.[67] Thus, state courts are sometimes more willing to hold some sale-and-lease-backs to be debt, depending on whether the building financed will produce market interest if the legislature opts out of its lease before the debt is paid.

An expansion of the concept of lease financing is subject-to-appropriation debt, or "contract debt," an invention of the closing decades of the 20th century.[68] Subject-to-appropriation debt uses the financing mechanism of lease financing but applies it to nonlease projects. Thus, a public authority will issue bonds in order to finance a project, and then it will enter into a contract with the legislature that calls for annual payments that are then used to pay the debt service. Just as in the case of lease-financing, the legislature is not obligated to appropriate the money called for in the contract, and most state courts have thus held that subject-to-appropriation financing is not debt.[69] Because of its nonobligatory nature, subject-to-appropriation borrowing is quite similar in nature to moral obligations borrowing.[70]

Subject-to-appropriation borrowing is widespread today, with a 2003 New Jersey case finding that at least 32 state courts had approved it.[71] Subject-to-appropriation financing has been criticized for its illusory nature, however. Although the legislature is not obligated to appropriate funds for debt service, the fact remains that failure to make payments on a bond can seriously impair a state or local government's credit rating and interest rates, making future bond issues difficult to market.[72] Therefore, when a government enters into a subject-to-appropriation agreement, it is unlikely that it will ever exercise its option not to appropriate the necessary funds. This is especially true when the project financed is not something that could be leased to a private party in case of default by the issuer, such as a highway or jail. In this regard, subject-to-appropriation debt appears to some to be a thinly veiled form of general obligation debt that nonetheless escapes the label of "debt." The frequency of defaults on this type of agreement has been described as "comparable to those of full faith and credit general obligation bonds."[73] Moreover, Standard & Poor's considers subject-to-appropriation borrowing to be a form of general obligation bond as a matter of policy.[74]

Some state courts have struggled to reconcile subject-to-appropriation debt with the explicit restraints of constitutional debt restriction provisions. For instance, in *Lonegan v. State*,[75] the New Jersey Supreme Court dealt with the issue of whether a literal reading of New Jersey's constitutional debt restriction provisions could be reconciled with the use of subject-to-appropriation debt, or whether allowing that method of borrowing notwithstanding the explicit restrictions of the state constitution "eviscerates the strictures of the Clause."[76] By a 4–3 vote, the court held that subject-to-appropriation debt was generally exempt from state and local debt restrictions.[77] This comports with the general rule that any type of borrowing that does not pledge the full faith and credit of the state, and that does not use the general taxing power of the state to pay debt service, is not debt.

As previously mentioned, the borrowing capacity of authorities has increasingly been used as a method of escaping state constitutional debt limitations. An authority is an "ad hoc unit of government" created for a single purpose of government, including to borrow and administer financed projects. There are two main categories of authorities. The first includes agencies, bureaus, boards, and commissions, all of which are "merely branches of such general purpose governments as cities, counties, and states."[78] The second main category is the special government, which includes special districts and public authorities. "Special governments are characterized by corporate organization, financial and operational independence, and jurisdictional flexibility."[79]

There are several differences between special districts and public authorities. Special districts are backed by the taxing power of the parent government and are financed by general obligation bonds or tax revenue.[80] Public authorities, on the other hand, are financed mainly by revenue bonds, particularly those issued to finance the project that the authority was created to administer.[81] Such authorities are not backed by the full taxing power of the parent government and they tend to be more independent.

By far the most popular form of special districts is the school district. However, such districts also exist for purposes of soil conservation, sewerage, drainage, fire protection, housing and urban renewal, water supply, and other governmental functions. Popular examples of public authorities include those for administration of transportation and the operation of public buildings.[82]

Special districts are often service-oriented and thus associated with the use of special assessments. Most courts have exempted the special assessment financing method from debt limitations. Indiana has been a leader in taking this view. That state recognizes "taxing districts," which are similar to special assessments and thus escape the debt moniker. Indiana therefore does not limit the number of bonds that will be repaid from revenues from special taxes.

Authorities may be created in one of three ways: "(1) through special act of the state legislature; (2) through a general act allowing counties and municipalities, singly or together, to create authorities; or (3) through a general act enabling the electorate of a defined region to approve their creation."[83] Authorities generally follow a "corporate pattern" (i.e., they are governed by a board of directors or commissioners, in much the same way as a private company).[84] Typically, authorities are given designated powers by the legislation that created them, including the power to sue and be sued, to borrow money and issue bonds, to issue subpoenas, to exercise the eminent domain power, and even to establish a police force.[85] As mentioned above, borrowing by authorities is typically excluded from constitutional debt limitations.[86] Further, if they are subject to debt restrictions, authorities are seen as being separate from their parent governments and thus as having their own debt, separate from the debts of the state, county, or municipality in which they provide services. Thus, where authorities overlap geographically, a large amount of debt capacity may legally be created.

One final financing mechanism that has become popular is the issuance of COPs. A COP is a security that represents an interest in payment that the issuer has promised to make but that is subject to annual appropriation by the state or local government. As such, COPs fall under the umbrella of subject-to-appropriation borrowing. The security is usually issued to finance a lease of real estate or equipment. Similar to a bond issue, a lessor transacting with a government entity may assign its interest to a third party who will provide funds. When the cost of a project is very high and multiple investors are required, the lessor may appoint a trustee to issue COPs signifying the portion of ownership assigned to each investor. In some circumstances, the certificates may be sold to institutional investors, or more easily to the public via underwriters.[87] COPs are considered municipal securities by the U.S. Securities and Exchange Commission under the registration and anti-fraud statutes.[88] Much like subject-to-appropriation borrowing, most courts have found that COPs are not unconstitutional debt since they are subject to annual appropriation.

Procedural Requirements for Local Government Debt Issuance Including Voter Approval by Referendum

Process Requirements for Issuing Local Government Debt

States have their own procedures for authorizing and issuing new debt that are usually set out in the state's constitution and statutes. Procedures for validating new debt issuance go beyond merely stating what sort of debt is allowable and the process for issuing new bonds. For example, some provisions require publication of the resolution authorizing the issuance of debt in case members of the public wish to oppose the locality's action. Care must be exercised in complying with these notification requirements since, in some instances, publication has been found to be insufficient by state courts. In *Ridenour v. County of Bay*,[89] for instance, the Supreme Court of Michigan held that two statutes requiring newspaper publication as notice of hearings of the county board of public works and bond validation proceedings violated the due process clause of the federal Constitution because they failed to give adequate notice. Generally, failure to comply with bond issuance procedures will result in the invalidation of the bond.

In other jurisdictions, local governments must obtain preapproval from state-level administrative agencies[90] or the state's attorney general prior to issuing debt.[91] In Louisiana and North Carolina this form of preclearance is mandated by constitutional provision.[92] Other states make this pre-issuance validation optional, however.

Citizen Approval of Debt through Bond Referenda

Many state law provisions mandate referenda and debt elections to approve the issuance of proposed bonds. Developed during the 19th century, public debt elections are intended to protect both residents and investors in municipal securities.[93] Referenda requirements usually apply to municipal debt offerings "that are secured by tax revenues or by the faith and credit of the issuer as opposed to the revenues of a self-sufficient project or one supported by a specially dedicated fund."[94] Usually, the definition of "debt" that is subject to the election or referendum requirement parallels the definition that applies to a state's debt limitations. All in all, this procedural approach makes a locality's decision to incur long-term debt a broadly democratic community choice, instead of simply an expedient decision of elected officials.[95]

These debt elections are frequently required to approve some, or in some cases all, borrowing by state and local governments.[96] A referendum is the process by which all eligible voters must vote to approve or confirm legislation enacted by a legislative body. Although the right to a referendum is not mandated by the federal Constitution,[97] many state, county, and local governments have granted the right under state law.[98] Moreover, the U.S. Supreme Court has invoked the equal protection clause of the Constitution to overturn state laws that selectively give the right to vote in a bond election to only a portion of eligible voters.

In *City of Phoenix v. Kolodziejski*,[99] the Court held that a city could not constitutionally exclude non–property owners from a referendum held to issue general obligation bonds.[100] Another case, *Cipriano v. City of Houma*,[101] came to a similar conclusion with facts considering revenue bonds.[102] And some U.S. Supreme Court precedents on the subject of voting have been employed by state courts to strike down state bond referendum requirements in ways that are arguably inconsistent with the Court's intent. For instance, the "one man, one vote" doctrine, distilled from landmark vote dilution cases like *Baker v. Carr*[103] and *Reynolds v. Sims*,[104] was applied by the Supreme Court of Appeals of West Virginia to reject a provision contained in the state constitution requiring a 60 percent super-majority approval before taxes could be levied in excess of the state's constitutional debt limit.[105] The state supreme court reversed a lower West Virginia court's decision that had concluded that the West Virginia Constitution did not discriminate against any "discrete and insular minority," and therefore did not violate the equal protection clause.[106]

Avoidance of the Referendum Requirement

Debt election provisions typically require the electorate to approve a proposed issuance of general obligation bonds.[107] Failure to obtain the approval of the electorate means the bonds will not be issued. At least 27 states require bond elections in order for municipalities to issue new debt.[108] Other states, such as Missouri and North Dakota, allow an increase of the debt limit by an additional percentage of assessed property if the electorate approves the addition.[109]

When a referendum is necessary, the issuer must be specific about the purpose of the bond issue. Failure to specify properly sometimes results in invalidation of the election. In *Schnoerr v. Miller*,[110] for instance, the Supreme Court of Ohio invalidated a bond election because the resolution to hold the election, the notice to voters, and the ballot itself stated only that the proceeds were to be used for a "public building," in contravention of a state statute requiring specificity. Moreover, the purpose stated in the notice, resolution, or ballot can be binding on the issuer. For example, in *Meyers v. Kansas City*,[111] the Supreme Court of Missouri affirmed an injunction preventing Kansas City from using bond proceeds to buy land on which to build a wharf since the election that approved the bonds stated that the proceeds would be used only to construct, improve, and buy equipment for docks and wharves.[112]

There are a number of restrictions on when referenda are applicable. Not surprisingly, states often attempt to invoke these exceptions to avoid the possibility of public denial of funds.[113] For example, governmental entities have often attempted to take refuge in the doctrine that referenda may be used in legislative but not administrative actions.[114] Administrative actions have been held to include purchasing land by a municipality; setting rates to be charged to service debt on revenue bonds; decisions on the city budget; and redevelopment agencies.[115] Legislative actions, on the other hand, have been held to include an amendment to a bond issue increasing the principal, and issuance of revenue bonds.[116] The distinction between these two kinds of actions, as can be readily perceived, is often difficult to comprehend.

In *Rauh v. Hutchinson*,[117] a Kansas court held that the act of implementing a statute was administrative in nature, delegated to the executing branch by the legislature. As such, execution of the ordinance in question was not subject to referendum. A similar approach was affirmed in *State Bond Commission v. All Taxpayers of Louisiana*,[118] where a Louisiana court held that the ability to issue RANs without a vote was constitutional.

Some courts have prohibited this type of evasion, though. In *Hot Springs v. Creviston*,[119] for instance, an Arkansas court overruled a prior case excepting revenue bonds from a public vote requirement. Though states differ in their judicial approaches to what sorts of acts must be submitted for electorate approval, in many states the line is a thin one. For example, in *Rauh*, the court set forth a set of guidelines aimed at distinguishing between administrative as opposed to legislative activities. The court said if an ordinance in question is one creating a new law or executing a currently existing one, it is legislative. If the act is permanent and general in nature, it is legislative. If the action is stated to have a public purpose or specifies methods of implementation, it is legislative. But actions requiring training and/or experience in municipal affairs are administrative.[120]

Referendum requirements also do not apply in other circumstances. Thus, voter approval of bond issues is typically not necessary where the subject matter is of a temporary and special character, where an essential governmental function may be impaired if debt financing is not used, where an emergency clause is attached to the enabling legislation, or where the enabling legislation is statewide in scope but the legislature has delegated implementing authority to a local governing board.

Notes

1. Letter from Thomas Jefferson to James Madison (Sept. 6, 1789), *reprinted in* The Portable Thomas Jefferson 444–51 (Merrill D. Peterson ed. 1975). Occasionally, a state court would echo this 18th-century sentiment. *See also* Dieck v. Unified Sch. Dist. of Antigo, 477 N.W.2d 613, 618 (Wis. 1991) (stating debt limits were intended to "limit the burden which those who contract obligations may place upon posterity").
2. The tax exemption of municipal bond interest has made these debt securities attractive to taxpayers in high marginal tax brackets.
3. *See* Pew Charitable Trusts, Defaulting on the Dream: States Respond to America's Foreclosure Crisis (2008), *available at* https://www.pewtrusts.org/-/media/assets/2008/04/16/defaulting_on_the_dream.pdf (identifying Connecticut, Delaware, Maryland, Massachusetts, Michigan, New Jersey, New York, Ohio, and Pennsylvania as having sold taxable bonds for this purpose).
4. *Id.*
5. *See* David Cho, *Municipal Bond Deals Squeezed by Credit Crisis*, Wash. Post, Nov. 29, 2007, at A1 (mentioning cancelled or postponed debt issues in Washington, D.C., Chicago, and south Florida).
6. Robert S. Amdursky & Clayton Gillette, Municipal Debt Finance Law 12–23 (1992).
7. M. David Gelfand, *Seeking Local Government Financial Integrity through Debt Ceilings, Tax Limitations, and Expenditure Limits: The New York City Fiscal Crisis, the Taxpayers' Revolt, and Beyond*, 63 Minn. L. Rev. 545, 546–51 (1979); A. James Heins, Constitutional Restrictions against State Debt 7–8 (1963); B.U. Ratchford, American State Debts 98–120 (1941).
8. Arthur Grinath III, John Joseph Wallis and Richard Sylla, *Debt Default and Revenue Structure: The American State Debt Crisis in the Early 1840s*, NBER Historical Paper No. 97, March 1997.
9. *See* Neil O'Hara, The Fundamentals of Municipal Bonds 55 (2012).
10. Some states have adopted legislation that comprehensively seeks to regulate government borrowing conduct and to avoid excessive state and local government debt. *See* Pennsylvania Debt Act, 53 Pa. Cons. Stat. Ann. §§ 8001–8271.

11. *See* Richard Briffault, *Foreword: The Disfavored Constitution: State Fiscal Limits and State Constitutional Law*, 34 RUTGERS L.J. 907, 915 (2003) (citing Stewart E. Sterk & Elizabeth S. Goldman, *Controlling Legislative Shortsightedness: The Effectiveness of Constitutional Debt Limitations*, 1991 WIS. L. REV. 1301, 1315 (1991)).
12. ADVISORY COMMISSION ON INTERGOVERNMENTAL RELATIONS, STATE TECHNICAL ASSISTANCE TO LOCAL DEBT MANAGEMENT 20, 21 (1965).
13. Briffault, *supra* note 11, at 918.
14. *E.g.*, Arkansas, Connecticut, and Nebraska.
15. KAN. CONST. art. IX, § 6 (delegating regulation of local government debt to the state legislature).
16. MD. CONST. art. III, §§ 54 & 34 (counties may not lend their credit, but the legislature may allow it under certain restrictions with an exception for emergency spending).
17. *See* M. DAVID GELFAND, STATE AND LOCAL GOVERNMENT DEBT FINANCING § 1:21 (2002).
18. Some states take other approaches restricting the amount of interest that local governments can pay for certain types of debt. MO. REV. STAT. § 108.170 (rates may not be > 14 percent per annum); MISS. CODE ANN. §§ 75-17-101, 75-17-103 (rates limited to 11 percent and 13 percent depending on type of municipal debt); ARK. CODE ANN. § 6-20-1206 (maximum rate may not exceed 5 percent of the Federal Reserve rate for primary credit); FLA. STAT. § 215.84(3) (rate may not exceed 300 basis points or 3 percent over "20 Bond Index" in *Bond Buyer*, but issuers can request exceptions from the State Board of Administration). Several states restrict the term or duration of local government debt. *See* CONN. GEN. STAT. § 7-273g(a) (40-year limit for transit debt); GA. CONST. art. IX, § V, para. 2 (30-year limit for special district debt); LA. REV. STAT. ANN. § 39:563 (40-year limit).
19. *E.g.*, Arizona, Kentucky, Maine, Ohio, and Rhode Island. *See* ARIZ. CONST. art. IX, §§ 5, 8 & 8.1; KY. CONST. § 158; ME. CONST. art. IX, § 14 & art. VIII, § 2; R.I. CONST. art. VI, § 16.
20. CAL. CONST. art. XVI, § 1.
21. WASH. CONST. art. VIII, § 1.
22. ARIZ. CONST. art. IX, § 5.
23. *E.g.*, ILL. CONST. art. IX, § 9(d) (limiting state debt to an amount not to exceed 15 percent of state appropriations for that fiscal year while excepting emergency spending from the debt limit).
24. *E.g.*, PA. CONST. art. VIII, § 7(a)(4) (1.75 times the average annual tax revenues for the prior five years); N.J. CONST. art. VIII, § 2 (1 percent of the amount appropriated by the legislature); HAW. CONST. art. VII, § 13 (18.5 percent of the prior three-year average of the state general fund revenues).
25. *E.g.*, NEV. CONST. art. IX, § 3 (caps state debt at 1 percent of assessed property value with exceptions); WY. CONST. §§ 1, 2, 3 & 5 (caps state debt at 1 percent of assessed property value with county debt limited to 2 percent of assessed property value).
26. IOWA CONST. art. XI (debt may not exceed 5 percent of taxable property). *See also* WIS. CONST. art XI, § 3 (debt may not exceed 5 percent of taxable property value with certain exceptions for school purposes).

27. VA. CONST. art. VII, § 10(a) (debt limited to 10 percent of assessed real property value).
28. MINN. STAT. § 475.53(3) (with other sections identifying exceptions).
29. LA. REV. STAT. ANN. §§ 33:2717.3, 39:562.
30. KY. CONST. § 158.
31. S.D. CONST. art. XIII, § 4.
32. *See* AMDURSKY & GILLETTE, *supra* note 6, § 4.3 n.4.
33. *See id.* n.6.
34. *See id.*
35. Limtiaco v. Camacho, 127 S. Ct. 1413 (2007).
36. *See* N.Y. CONST. art. VIII, § 5(b).
37. *E.g.*, Florida, South Carolina, South Dakota, Utah, Washington, and Wyoming.
38. *E.g.*, Arizona, Indiana, Iowa, Maine, New Jersey, North Carolina, Pennsylvania, Rhode Island, and Wyoming.
39. *E.g.*, New Jersey and Pennsylvania.
40. IDAHO CONST. art. VIII, § 3. *See also* GELFAND, *supra* note 17, § 3:04.
41. *See* GELFAND, *supra* note 17, § 3:04.
42. *See id.* n.6.
43. *See* Briffault, *supra* note 11, at 918–27.
44. *See, e.g.*, IDAHO CONST. art. VIII, § 3; Pocatello v. Peterson, 473 P.2d 644 (Idaho 1970) (finding that expenditures for construction of expanded airport facilities not debt because "ordinary" and "necessary").
45. *See, e.g.*, Los Angeles County v. Byram, 227 P.2d 4 (Cal. 1951); Hillcrest Med. Ctr. v. State *ex rel.* Dep't of Corr., 675 P.2d 432 (Okla. 1983); Goff v. City of Seattle, 86 P.2d 222 (Wash. 1939).
46. *See* AMDURSKY & GILLETTE, *supra* note 6, § 4.4.
47. *See* GELFAND, *supra* note 17, § 3:04 n.6.
48. *See Byram*, 227 P.2d 4.
49. AMDURSKY & GILLETTE, *supra* note 6, § 4.4 nn.12–14, 16.
50. *See id.* n.24.
51. *See id.* n.25.
52. *See id.* n.22.
53. *See* Briffault, *supra* note 11, at 919.
54. *See* M. DAVID GELFAND ET AL., STATE AND LOCAL TAXATION AND FINANCE 104–14 (3d ed. 2007).
55. *See, e.g.*, *In re* Okla. Capitol Improvement Auth., 958 P.2d 759 (Okla. 1998) (holding that bonds issued to finance new highways were not debt because the new road would increase auto usage while being subjected to an additional fuel tax as well as fees); Convention Ctr. Auth. v. Anzai, 890 P.2d 1197 (Haw. 1995) (holding that a convention center financed with public bonds did not create debt because a new tax on hotels, coupled with the increased tourism created by the convention center, would create sufficient revenue to pay the debt service). *But see* Eakin v. State *ex rel.* Capital Improvement Bd., 474 N.E.2d 62, 67 (Ind. 1985) (holding that bond used to finance a convention center and backed by taxes on hotels, motels, and retail food business is "debt" within the meaning of debt limit).

56. State *ex rel.* Council of City of Charleston v. Hall, 441 S.E.2d 386 (W. Va. 1994) (holding that long-term contract for garbage disposal not considered debt when contract fees payable solely from charges paid by residents for refuse disposal).
57. *See, e.g.*, Loomis v. Keehn, 80 N.E.2d 368, 371 (Ill. 1948).
58. *See* GELFAND, *supra* note 17, § 3:04.
59. *See* City of Los Angeles v. Offner, 122 P.2d 14 (Cal. 1942); Montano v. Gabaldon, 766 P.2d 1328, 1330 (N.M. 1989); GELFAND, *supra* note 17, § 3:04 n.15.
60. *See generally* Robert H. Bowmar, *The Anachronism Called Debt Limitation*, 52 IOWA L. REV. 863 (1967).
61. *See* GELFAND, *supra* note 17, § 1:22 nn.16 & 17.
62. The courts are divided on this topic. Iowa, Missouri, and Colorado cases have struck down such arrangements, but California, Iowa, and South Dakota cases have ruled in favor.
63. A New Jersey case, for instance, held that similarity between a lease and an installment contract was not crucial to the actual status, rather whether the contract was "defensible theoretically" as a lease. Bulman v. McCrane, 312 A.2d 857, 861 (N.J. 1993). California courts have found leases to be *bona fide* when they include provisions for automatic transfer of title to the city upon last payment. In *Dean v. Kuchel*, 218 P.2d 521 (Cal. 1950), the court said there was no "substantial or logical difference" between an option to purchase at the end of a rental period and an automatic title transfer at the end of the period. *See also* Ruane v. City of San Diego, 73 Cal. Rptr. 316 (Cal. Ct. App. 1968); *Bulman*, 312 A.2d 857; Mun. Bldg. Auth. of Iron County v. Lowder, 711 P.2d 273 (Utah 1985).
64. Briffault, *supra* note 11, at 919.
65. *See id.*
66. *See id.* at 920.
67. *See* Montano v. Gabaldon, 766 P.2d 1328 (N.M. 1989).
68. *See* Briffault, *supra* note 11, at 920.
69. *See* Carr-Gottstein Props. v. State, 899 P.2d 136 (Alaska 1995); *In re* Anzai, 936 P.2d 637 (Haw. 1997); Wilson v. Ky. Transp. Cabinet, 884 S.W.2d 641 (Ky. 1994); Employers Ins. Co. of Nev. v. State Bd. of Exam'rs, 21 P.3d 628 (Nev. 2001); Schulz v. State, 639 N.E.2d 1140 (N.Y. 1994); Fent v. Okla. Capitol Improvement Auth., 984 P.2d 200 (Okla. 1999); Dykes v. N. Va. Transp. Dist. Comm'n, 411 S.E.2d 1 (Va. 1991).
70. *See* Briffault, *supra* note 11, at 921.
71. *See* Lonegan v. State, 819 A.2d 395, 404 n.2 (N.J. 2003) (*Lonegan II*).
72. *See* Briffault, *supra* note 11, at 923.
73. *See id.* at 922.
74. *See id.* (citing Richard J. Marino & Colleen Waddell, *Revised Lease and Appropriation-Backed Debt*, STANDARD & POOR'S RATING SERVICES, June 13, 2001).
75. Lonegan v. State, 809 A.2d 91 (N.J. 2002).
76. *See id.* at 93.
77. *See Lonegan II*, 819 A.2d 395, 407 (N.J. 2003).
78. *See* Comment, *An Analysis of Authorities: Traditional and Multicounty*, 71 MICH. L. REV. 1376, 1377 (1973).

79. *See id.*
80. *See id.* at 1378.
81. *See id.*
82. *See id.*
83. *See id.* at 1377, 1380.
84. *See id.*
85. *See id.* at 1381.
86. *See id.* at 1398. *See also* Kennebec Water Dist. v. City of Waterville, 52 A. 774 (Me. 1902).
87. *See* GELFAND, *supra* note 17, § 3:25.
88. *See id.* § 3:26.
89. Ridenour v. County of Bay, 114 N.W.2d 172, 178–80 (Mich. 1962).
90. In Pennsylvania, review and approval of proposed bond issues is the responsibility of the Pennsylvania Department of Community Affairs. *See* N. Pocono Taxpayers Ass'n v. Commonwealth, 625 A.2d 1343 (Pa. Commw. Ct. 1993).
91. *See* Barbara Klickinger & Katherine McManus, *Bankruptcy Aftershocks: Have Public Finance Foundations Been Shaken?*, 78 PUB. MGMT. 1 (1996) (discussing control boards for New York, Cleveland, Yonkers, Bridgeport and New Haven, Connecticut, and Chicago).
92. LA. CONST. art. VI, § 33 and N.C. CONST. art. V, § 4(2). Other states require this procedure through statutes. *See* NEV. REV. STAT. §§ 350.0115, 350.014 (2001).
93. In recent years, efforts were undertaken to eliminate the debt referendum requirement most often when school bonds were at issue. In addition, some creative alternatives to bond financing have been deemed to be beyond the reach of the referendum requirement. *See* GELFAND, *supra* note 17, § 9.06.
94. AMDURSKY & GILLETTE, *supra* note 6, at 60.
95. *See* Tracy Nichols Eddy, *The Referendum Requirement: A Constitutional Limitation on Local Government Debt in Florida*, 38 U. MIAMI L. REV. 677 (1984); David B. Magleby, *Let the Voters Decide? An Assessment of the Initiative and Referendum Process*, 66 U. COLO. L. REV. 13 (1995).
96. It has been noted that several state constitutions require a majority vote in a local election or referendum held prior to the issuance of local government debt using this method as "a complete substitute for a substantive debt ceiling." GELFAND, *supra* note 17, § 9.06.
97. *See, e.g.*, Lee v. Comm'rs Court of Jefferson County, 81 F. Supp. 2d 712 (E.D. Tex. 2000).
98. California, for instance, reserves to the people the power of referendum in its constitution, CAL. CONST. art IV, § 1. *See generally* GELFAND, *supra* note 17, § 1:15.
99. City of Phoenix v. Kolodziejski, 399 U.S. 204 (1970).
100. *Id.* at 214. It should be noted, however, that the Court's holding in this case was based on the rationale that the payment source for the bonds was not solely property taxes, and that default on the bonds would have an impact on both owners and nonowners alike. This begs the question of whether the Court would rule in the same way if ownership of property was required to participate in an election where the sole source of payment for the bonds was property taxes.

101. Cipriano v. City of Houma, 395 U.S. 701 (1969).
102. *Id.* at 702.
103. Baker v. Carr, 369 U.S. 186 (1962).
104. Reynolds v. Sims, 377 U.S. 533 (1964).
105. *See* Lance v. Bd. of Educ., 170 S.E.2d 783 (W. Va. 1969).
106. *See* Gordon v. Lance, 403 U.S. 1, 4 (1971).
107. *See* AMDURSKY & GILLETTE, *supra* note 6, § 2.4.
108. *See* ALA. CONST. art. XII, § 222; ALASKA CONST. art. IX, § 9; ARIZ. CONST. art. VII, § 13, art. IX, § 8; ARK. CONST. amend. 62, § 1; CAL. CONST. art. XVI, § 18; COLO. CONST. art. XI, § 6; FLA. CONST. art. VII, § 12; GA. CONST. art. IX, § 5; IDAHO CONST. art. VIII, § 3; LA. CONST. art. VI, §§ 7, 14, 33 & 35; MD. CONST. art. 11-E, § 5; MICH. CONST. art. IX, § 25; MO. CONST. art. VI, § 26; NEB. CONST. art. XIII, § 2; N.M. CONST. art. IX, § 12; N.C. CONST. art. V, § 4; N.D. CONST. art. X, § 15; OKLA. CONST. art. X, §§ 26 & 27B; OR. CONST. art. XI, § 11; PA. CONST. art. IX, § 10 (for bonds in excess of debt limit); S.C. CONST. art. XVII, § 7B; S.D. CONST. art. XIII, § 4; TEX. CONST. art. III, § 52; UTAH CONST. art. XIV, § 7; VA. CONST. art. VII, § 10; WASH. CONST. art. VIII, § 6; W. VA. CONST. art. X, § 8. *See also* Clayton P. Gillette, *Direct Democracy and Debt*, 13 J. CONTEMP. LEGAL ISSUES 365, 370–71 (2004).
109. *See generally supra* note 108.
110. Schnoerr v. Miller, 206 N.E.2d 902 (Ohio 1965).
111. Meyers v. Kansas City, 18 S.W.2d 900 (Mo. 1929).
112. *Id.* at 901.
113. *See* GELFAND, *supra* note 17, § 1:15.
114. *See id.*
115. *See id.* n.23.
116. *See id.*
117. Rauh v. Hutchinson, 575 P.2d 517 (Kan. 1978).
118. State Bond Comm'n v. All Taxpayers of La., 510 So. 2d 662 (La. 1987).
119. Hot Springs v. Creviston, 705 S.W.2d 415 (Ark. 1986).
120. *See Rauh*, 575 P.2d at 522–23.

6

Regulation of Municipal Securities

The Origins of U.S. Regulation of the Securities Market

Securities have been essential to the growth and development of the United States throughout its history by providing the necessary capital for private-sector and governmental physical expansion. They represent the means that firms and governmental units employ to finance the costs of developing necessary land and structures. Securities are sold to investors either as a way of giving them an equity stake in a corporate venture or else as debt serving as a loan of money to be repaid at a future time with interest. Debt securities or bonds essentially represent promissory notes containing a promise from the borrower to repay the loan under specified terms. The value of a bond depends upon the creditworthiness of the borrower (called the issuer) and its ability to service and, ultimately, pay off the debt in the future. All financial securities ask investors to assume variable levels of risk with their investment dollars and they look to future return of the invested funds with interest and possible capital appreciation. Securities are also goods that are complex. They are often difficult for potential buyers to evaluate and assess. This may be due to the information asymmetry between the issuer of the security and the investor as well as uncertainty regarding future events. In the past, the complexity of investments in securities has given rise to a fertile field for fraudulent marketing and deceptive sales practices by original sellers, as well as subsequent traders, who have taken advantage of purchasers' lack of accurate information and lack of sophistication. As the discussion below will explain, federal securities law in the 20th and 21st centuries has developed with an emphasis on the provision of information to investors when they are contemplating the purchase and sale of securities.

An Overview of Federal Securities Law

Historical Background

American securities law grew out of the period following the stock market crash of 1929. During his campaign for the presidency in 1932, Franklin D. Roosevelt promised sweeping legislative reforms that would protect citizens from the severe economic effects of a speculative financial industry that had broken down and left the nation in economic turmoil. At that time, the rate of unemployment exceeded 23 percent and the value of investment securities had fallen 50 percent over a three-year period. After his landslide victory, President Roosevelt sponsored a number of statutes that now form the central structure of federal securities law. One of his first acts as president was to assemble an outstanding drafting group (including Felix Frankfurter, James Landis, Thomas Corcoran, and Benjamin Cohen) that would develop the ideas and legislative language of what Congress passed as the Securities Act of 1933 (generally known as "the 1933 Act").[1] This law first established a comprehensive regulatory system affecting the public offering of securities. Its main focus was to discourage fraudulent and deceptive practices by (1) requiring that a securities regulatory statement be registered with the federal government (at first with the Federal Trade Commission and later with the U.S. Securities and Exchange Commission (SEC)); (2) mandating the disclosure of material information in a prospectus prior to offering securities for sale; and (3) prohibiting the release of inaccurate information in the sale or offering of securities. These requirements were enforced by a range of private and public enforcement mechanisms.

In the next year, the Securities Exchange Act was enacted (generally known as "the 1934 Act" or "the Exchange Act").[2] That statute established the SEC and provided for the SEC regulation of securities trading and for the operation of securities resale or secondary markets. The 1934 Act also regulated the stock exchanges and securities firms, prohibited deceptive or manipulative marketing practices, required periodic disclosure by public companies, and regulated insider trading. The Exchange Act has been amended a number of times since 1934 and these amendments have extended the reach of this act well beyond that of the original legislation. As an area of practice, securities law is highly specialized, requiring extensive expertise and familiarity with applicable case law, statutes, regulations, and other legal materials.

Statutory Purposes

The main thrust of both the 1933 and the 1934 Acts was to promote the disclosure of relevant investment information to investors, and thereby create a more equal informational playing field for investors. The acts' "disclosure" philosophy rejected an alternative "merit regulation" approach that would have authorized a governmental agency to judge the merit of investments, giving it the power to bar investments determined to fall short of qualitative standards. The 1933 and 1934 statutes—along with regulations that implement their provisions—continue to form the central core of federal securities regulation. However, the remaining half of the 1930s also saw the enactment of four more statutes dealing with more specialized securities problems. Within this expanded statutory structure, the 1933 Act requires the SEC to review securities marketed in interstate commerce issues before they are offered or sold through the filing of registration statements. In addition, section 11 of the 1933 Act imposes liability on certain persons for misstatements or omissions of a material fact from a registration statement.

The Developing Federal Statutory Policy Governing State or Municipal Securities

Basic Coverage of Federal Law

State and local government securities were initially considered to be "exempt securities," excluded from both the registration requirements of the 1933 Act[3] and the reporting requirements of the 1934 Act.[4] Congress believed that sophisticated parties invested in municipal securities and that these securities did not present the same level of danger to investors as had been recognized in corporate financial investments. In addition, serious questions existed concerning the constitutional authority of Congress to regulate the financial operations of state and local governments. As a result, securities issued by municipalities are not subject to the registration requirements of the 1933 Act; but they do fall under the anti-fraud provisions of that statute and the 1934 Act.

Both of these important federal securities laws share a common set of purposes: (1) requiring disclosure of information allowing investors to inform themselves before investing and (2) prohibiting fraud in the securities industry. Over the years, the anti-fraud provisions of these statutes have been interpreted and applied in numerous court cases, which have provided a significant judicial gloss on the 1933 and 1934 Acts. A discussion of the most salient legal issues related to these two statutes will follow below. This discussion will also treat some further amendments to these laws that Congress has enacted in recent years.

Congress passed the Securities Investor Protection Act of 1970,[5] the Securities Acts Amendments of 1975,[6] and the Sarbanes-Oxley Act of 2002,[7] which adopted comprehensive corporate governance reforms. The 1975 Securities Acts Amendments established a regulatory regime for the dealers and brokers of municipal securities. In 1990, the SEC issued Rule 15c2-12, which regulates the timing and production of disclosure documents by the brokers, dealers, and underwriters of municipal securities; and in 1995, the SEC amended the rule to provide for secondary market disclosure rules.

The Increasing Importance of Disclosure in Municipal Finance Law

Prior to the 1970s, disclosure was not a major concern for municipal securities, and only limited requirements as to disclosure were imposed under securities law. As a result, municipal bond issuers, often marketing bonds backed by their full faith and credit securing timely payment, generally disclosed only limited information about the bond itself and the entity issuing the debt. The securities abuses that had led to the enactment of the 1933 and 1934 Acts—and the imposition of the registration and periodic information disclosure requirements—had been mainly associated with corporate, not municipal, securities. In the last quarter of the 20th century, however, the municipal bond market significantly changed with respect to both the volume of financing transactions and the complexity of municipal financing. These market changes ultimately led to the important changes in the law discussed below.

Financial Crisis and Municipal Securities

New York City has frequently been at the center of financial crises centered upon municipal debt. In fact, Tammany Hall boss William Tweed was actually brought down by the financial crisis of 1871 and Mayor Fiorello LaGuardia narrowly protected the city during the Depression of the 1930s from declaring municipal bankruptcy. In 1975, New York City encountered a similar financial crisis—a crisis so severe that by April of that year the city came close to being unable to meet its payroll and to make payments for ordinary city operations. While admitting to an operating budget shortfall of at least $600 million (with some estimates as high as $2.2 billion), the city drew close to total financial meltdown when it nearly defaulted on $14 billion of outstanding long- and short-term debt. Coordinated efforts of New York State and of the federal government were needed to temporarily lend the city billions of dollars and assist it in reducing its spending and managing the shortfall. It was not until 1981 that New York City was able to sell long-term bonds once again, and to operate with a balanced budget that followed generally accepted accounting principles.[8]

The New York City crisis was followed on the West Coast in 1983 by the default of the Washington Public Power Supply System (WPPSS) on bonds that had been issued to finance a series of five nuclear power plants in the Pacific Northwest. In that year, the WPPSS became infamous for defaulting on $2.25 billion worth of bonds after construction on two of its nuclear power plants was halted. The default remains the largest municipal bond default in the history of the United States, acquiring the nickname "whoops" in the financial media. As of 2008, about 15 percent of the residential electric bill receipts collected by participating public utilities still went to paying principal and interest on the abandoned plants.[9]

These financial debacles, in conjunction with several other less prominent yet similar events, brought greater public and governmental attention to municipal debt securities. Ultimately, that attention resulted in increased regulation of the industry. Courts began to more actively find violations of the anti-fraud statutory provisions and the SEC started to pursue enforcement actions. These developments, in turn, have led to the preparation of "official statements," documents accompanying modern government bond issues, which are comparable to the prospectuses used for registered corporate securities offerings. They have also given rise to additional SEC regulations and to the creation of the Municipal Securities Rulemaking Board (MSRB) in 1975.[10]

The MSRB is an independent rulemaking body that oversees the municipal securities industry. Its rules, commonly known as "fair practice rules," prohibit brokers and dealers from engaging in fraudulent or manipulative acts and practices.[11] Although MSRB rules are said to have the force of law, the board may not enforce them. Instead, that task falls to the SEC, the National Association of Securities Dealers (NASD), and federal banking agencies.

Constitutional Limits to the Regulation of Municipal Securities Issuers

One fundamental issue concerning the federal regulation of state and local government issuers of securities relates to the power of Congress to authorize such regulation under the U.S. Constitution. Focusing principally on the intergovernmental immunity concepts contained within the Tenth Amendment,[12] states have argued that the federal government could not constitutionally intrude into core state activities or functions without unduly interfering with essential state sovereignty. The U.S. Supreme Court's 1976 opinion in *National League of Cities v. Usery*[13] relied on the Tenth Amendment to invalidate the extension of the federal Fair Labor Standards Act to many state and local government employees. The principal rationale for this outcome was the notion that the federal law at issue would interfere with state and municipal budgeting and the setting of spending priorities, thereby interfering with traditional governmental activities. This case overruled the 1968 holding in *Maryland v. Wirtz*, which had upheld the constitutionality of federal minimum wage and overtime pay rules as applied to states and local government workers.[14] The *National League of Cities* decision suggested that federal rules that increased state and local government financial costs in providing these "inherent" or "integral" functions might conflict with the Tenth Amendment. In the municipal bond area, following *National League of Cities*, federal securities law regulations that had the effect of increasing basic capital fundraising costs became legally suspect and potentially violative of the Tenth Amendment.

This concern soon dissipated, however. Several subsequent decisions addressed the issue of Tenth Amendment state immunity and the application of federal securities law. For example, in *Woods v. Homes & Structures of Pittsburg, Kansas, Inc.*, an industrial development bond issue entered default and the issuer raised a Tenth Amendment defense against federal securities law claims. That defense was rejected on the basis that such bonds did not "rise to the level of a traditional governmental function."[15]

The impact of the *National League of Cities* decision was brief, however. By 1985, the Supreme Court reversed itself with its holding in *Garcia v. San Antonio Metropolitan Transit Authority*,[16] which overruled *National League of Cities*, finding it to be "unworkable" in establishing the limits of state immunity for "traditional governmental functions." Although theoretically recognizing limits to federal authority, the *Garcia* Court left it to the political branches of government to establish the actual boundaries between federal regulation and state autonomy. In the Supreme Court's view, the concept of federalism was to find its defense through the political process, and not in the courts.

In a more recent decision in *New York v. United States*, the Court ruled that a federal hazardous waste law constituted a commandeering of state authority in support of a federal legislative objective that violated constitutional limits.[17] However, the statute under review in that case was specifically focused on states rather than being more general in nature. This suggests that federal securities laws may be safe from constitutional challenge due to their general regulatory nature, and to the fact that they do not solely target state and municipal financial operations.

Federal Securities Law Anti-Fraud Provisions and Their Application to Municipal Securities

As noted above, the original federal securities legislation focused on the twin objectives of requiring the disclosure of material information about securities and banning misrepresentation or fraud in the marketing of securities. Although municipal bond issues were initially made exempt from the registration requirements, they are still subject to the anti-fraud provisions of both the 1933 and 1934 Acts. Many provisions of federal securities law are highly detailed and specific in providing grounds for highly articulated regulations or other rules governing particular transactions or marketing practices. It is therefore highly recommended that specialized research be done for specific legal and policy questions.[18] At any rate, the statutory basis for the applicable anti-fraud provisions can be found in four statutory sections and one SEC regulation: section 17, section 11, and section 12(2) of the 1933 Act, section 10(b) of the 1934 Act, and Rule 10b-5 promulgated by the SEC. These critical statutory and regulatory provisions, and their judicial construction, are described below.

The Securities Act of 1933

Section 17(a)

Section 5 of the 1933 Act mandates that securities issued for sale in interstate commerce have a registration statement filed with the SEC prior to being offered for sale. This fundamental registration requirement is subject to certain exceptions and one of these pertains to the sale of municipal or state bonds. Section 3(a)(2) of that act exempts any security that is issued or guaranteed by a state, a political subdivision, or a public instrumentality. It also applies to industrial development bonds.[19] As a result of these statutory exemptions, section 17(a) is the only substantive provision of the 1933 Act to directly apply to municipal securities.

Section 17(a) makes it unlawful in the offer or sale of any securities in interstate commerce for a person to "use any device, scheme, or artifice to defraud," to make "any untrue statement of material fact or any omission to state a material fact" that was misleading, or to engage in a "fraud or deceit upon the purchaser." That statutory language is nearly identical to the wording of SEC Rule 10b-5 to be discussed later. However, under the terms of section 17(a), the statute only prohibits the listed conduct in connection with the "offer or sale" of securities. Therefore, only buyers of securities who have been defrauded may bring actions under this section. In contrast, SEC Rule 10b-5 applies to *both* buyers and sellers of securities. Due to the breadth of its coverage, Rule 10b-5 has been more frequently used to litigate cases of alleged securities fraud, especially after the courts determined that private lawsuits could be brought under its terms.[20]

In the mid-1970s, the U.S. Supreme Court's decision in *Blue Chip Stamps v. Manor Drug Stores*[21] read Rule 10b-5 narrowly, requiring the plaintiff to clearly establish standing to sue and to demonstrate that the defendant had acted with the intent or knowledge of its wrongdoing. This element is known in the law as "scienter."[22] In *Aaron v. SEC*,[23] the Supreme Court analyzed the statutory text and ruled that the SEC must prove that the defendant acted with scienter in its civil enforcement suits brought under parts of section 17(a). However, the wrongful knowledge required for section 17(a)(1) was not found necessary for enforcement against violations of section 17(a)(2) and (3). This difference created the possibility that suits might be brought by the SEC and private parties both for knowing noncompliance and for negligent violations of the 1933 Act. In view of the breadth of section 17(a)—which expressly prohibits fraud, deception, and manipulation, as well as misstatements and omissions—the provision holds great potential as a remedial and policing tool for the securities industry, including sellers of municipal bonds.

An important question has arisen as to which procedures would be available to enforce the terms of the 1933 Act. More specifically, is section 17(a) to be enforced exclusively by the federal securities regulatory agency, the SEC, or would private individuals have a similar right as well? Investor-initiated litigation is (at least potentially) an important adjunct to federal enforcement efforts. However, the legal status of this mechanism is tenuous. Although the statute does not contain an explicit provision granting the private right of action, lower federal courts had implied a private cause of action since 1949.[24] Unfortunately, the Supreme Court has not confirmed this interpretation, and the U.S. Circuit Courts of Appeals have split on the question. Thus, currently, although the majority of courts of appeals do not recognize such an implied cause of action in the courts,[25] federal case law takes regrettably inconsistent positions as to whether to allow private lawsuits to enforce the provisions of section 17(a) of the 1933 Act.[26]

The Due Diligence Defense under Sections 11 and 12(2) of the 1933 Act

The 1933 Act generally requires that, absent a statutory exemption, the filing of a registration statement with the SEC must precede the offer or sale of securities. This disclosure requirement was intended to provide buyers of securities with accurate and universally available information about financial products whose purchase they are considering. In order to enforce this policy, section 11 allows the purchaser of a security to sue if there is a false statement or an omission of material fact in the registration statement. Under section 11, issuers of securities are strictly liable, while other parties involved in the transaction, such as bond counsel and underwriter's counsel, are subject to a negligence standard.

Since municipal securities are exempted from the registration requirements of the 1933 Act, section 11 does not directly apply to municipal securities, which are considered exempt transactions. However, the SEC has determined that even parties involved in exempt transactions are under a duty to make a reasonable investigation and to have reasonable grounds to believe that statements made were accurate and complete. This is known as the "due diligence" requirement, and it requires the degree of reasonableness of a "prudent man in the management of his own property."[27] Nonetheless, section 12(2) of the 1933 Act does establish a federal cause of action for a purchaser of a security against a person who offers or sells the security in interstate commerce by way of a false prospectus or oral communications, whether or not the security in question is exempt from the registration requirement of the act.

The Securities Exchange Act of 1934

Section 10(b)

Section 10(b) of the 1934 Act makes it unlawful for any person using the mail or interstate commerce to use manipulative or deceptive practices related to the purchase or sale of securities "in contravention" of rules adopted by the SEC. In 1942, the SEC adopted Rule 10b-5, which was intended to carry out the policy of section 10(b). Rule 10b-5 makes it unlawful for a person to (1) employ any device, scheme, or artifice to defraud; (2) make any untrue statement of a material fact or omit to state a material fact necessary in order to make the statements made not misleading; or (3) to engage in any act, practice, or course of business that operates or would operate as a fraud or deceit upon any person, in connection with the purchase or sale of any security. Notably, Rule 10b-5 focuses on the sale of securities, providing a private cause of action for damages applicable to a range of actors in securities transactions. Section 10(b) and Rule 10b-5 have been used by both the SEC and private litigants to enforce the anti-fraud policies of both the federal securities statute and the regulation.

The basic structure of Rule 10b-5 has required proof of the customary elements of a common law fraud claim. The focus has been on four principal elements: (1) a misstatement or omission of a material fact; (2) an intent to deceive, manipulate, or defraud (i.e., scienter); (3) reliance by the plaintiff on the misstatement or omission; and (4) damages suffered as a result of the plaintiff's reliance. It should be noted that this rule has also been invoked against fraudulent schemes, artifices, and devices, which have led to allegations of market manipulation as well.[28] These general elements, which are contained in both the rule and the statute, have been more precisely defined in the numerous case decisions that have followed.

Since 1955, Rule 10b-5 has been judicially held to apply to municipal bonds; this coverage was made clear by a statutory codification in the 1970s. The Securities Act Amendments of 1975,[29] the first federal regulatory scheme addressing the municipal securities market, expressly made Rule 10b-5 applicable to municipal issuers by expanding the definition of "person" in section 3(a)(9) of the amendments to include "a government, or political subdivision, agency or instrumentality of a government." The Ninth Circuit confirmed the meaning of this section in the *Washington Public Power Supply System Securities Litigation* case in 1987.[30]

Furthermore, even though Rule 10b-5 does not contain a private remedy provision, the U.S. Supreme Court ruled in *Superintendent of Insurance v. Bankers Life & Casualty Co*. that an implied private cause of action exists under Rule 10b-5, and subsequent federal court decisions ruled that such an action might be brought against municipalities.[31] Plaintiffs must prove the elements of their case by a preponderance of the evidence.[32] The U.S. Supreme Court also determined that standing to sue is available to parties who buy or sell securities at the time that a fraud occurs.[33]

As described below, the four elements of the Rule 10b-5 test have received significant interpretation in court decisions. These judicial rulings have also provided glosses to the general language of the rule.

Misstatement or Omission of a Material Fact

SEC Rule 10b-5 bans factual misstatements and omissions of material facts as the focus of its anti-fraud policy. It is "material" facts, not all facts about the issuer or the issue, that must be truthfully disclosed. But what constitutes a misstatement and what is an omission? These have been perplexing and frequently litigated questions in American securities law, and the SEC has been increasingly concerned about omissions and misstatements made by bond issuers in informational statements. Occasionally, the questions arise in the context of an omission of certain facts that makes the disclosed statements misleading in the circumstances under which they were made. Even partial omissions can be deemed significant if the fact omitted is considered to be "material."

As previously stated, Rule 10b-5 only requires the disclosure of accurate information that is "material."[34] Misrepresentations and omissions have been defined as "material" in U.S. Supreme Court decisions when a reasonable investor would consider the information important in deciding whether to invest[35]—that is, information that would have been influential in investment decisions. Rule 10b-5 also requires that misstated or omitted information must have caused an investor's financial losses. Cases like *Robbins v. Koger Properties* have required that the plaintiff in a Rule 10b-5 action prove that the failure of disclosure caused both the investment to occur and the value to decline.[36]

Determining whether certain information is material depends, to a significant extent, upon the context and nature of the investment transaction. With municipal bond issues, the definition of material information will depend upon the nature of the financed activity, the creditworthiness of the issuer, and the streams of debt service payments that were to be available to service the debt. Thus, determining the materiality of undisclosed or misstated information will almost always depend upon the facts and circumstances of the situation.

An Intent to Deceive, Manipulate, or Defraud Plaintiff

An important question that has arisen in litigation enforcing Rule 10b-5 concerns the standard for liability in a private party action for damages. Can mere negligence be the basis for such an allegation or is clear evidence of fraudulent intent required? In *Ernst & Ernst v. Hochfelder*,[37] the U.S. Supreme Court resolved this issue by concluding that the plaintiff in a Rule 10b-5 action must prove scienter in the defendant's actions in order to recover[38]—that is, "a mental state embracing an intent to deceive, manipulate or defraud."[39] The proof must establish knowing or intentional conduct on the part of the wrongdoer. The implication of the *Hochfelder* decision was that merely negligent conduct would not be sufficient grounds for a Rule 10b-5 private enforcement action. Left unresolved in *Hochfelder* was the question of whether "reckless" behavior could support such an action. The U.S. Supreme Court has yet to speak on this question. However, the federal circuit courts of appeals have uniformly indicated that recklessness does satisfy the scienter requirement;[40] and this interpretation of Rule 10b-5 appears to apply regardless of whether or not a private party is bringing a damage action or the SEC is seeking injunctive relief.[41]

Reliance by Plaintiff upon Defendant's Misstatement or Omission

Rule 10b-5 usually requires that the plaintiff establish a causal link between an alleged misstatement or omission and a financial injury. The concept of reliance establishes that connection. Reliance is said to have two elements: (1) the plaintiff must have actual knowledge of the defendant's misstatement, and (2) the plaintiff's belief in the truth of the misstatement must have been a cause of the plaintiff's participation in the financial transaction. The plaintiff's reliance must also have been reasonable, as demonstrated by due diligence on the part of each plaintiff in an action. In some cases, reliance has been found to be unjustified where the risks involved were obvious or well known and the plaintiff did not take steps to investigate or assess the risks.

Misstatements are one thing. Omissions present a somewhat different problem. It seems difficult, if not impossible, to prove reliance on the absence of information through nondisclosure as the causative element in a fraud case. The U.S. Supreme Court recognized this and suggested, in *Affiliated Ute Citizens v. United States*,[42] that in factual omission cases, reliance will be presumed from the plaintiff's demonstration of materiality of the omission, and that this presumption may be rebutted by the defendant.[43] Some lower federal court cases have also followed this approach.[44]

A presumption of reliance has not been applied in cases of misstatement of fact or inaccurate information.[45] However, even where a plaintiff cannot prove that it has relied on a defendant's misstatements or omissions, the plaintiff may still base a claim by relying upon the theory of "fraud on the market." Under this theory, on the assumption that the market evaluates material information regarding securities, a fraud may be found when the defendant's actions have the effect of artificially affecting a security's price. In such a case, causation of a plaintiff's financial injury may be presumed. The U.S. Supreme Court has supported this "fraud on the market" view in well-developed markets in the *Basic Inc. v. Levinson* decision, a ruling that is consistent with Rule 10b-5 and the policy underlying the 1934 Act.[46]

Damages Suffered by Plaintiff as a Result of Its Reliance

In most cases under Rule 10b-5, the plaintiff is seeking damages as its principal remedy. This aspect of Rule 10b-5 has largely been the creation of the courts, since the SEC rule does not specifically mention damages. The 1934 Act limits the plaintiff's recovery to "actual damages," and the U.S. Supreme Court has ruled that the act is the correct measure of damages for Rule 10b-5 violations.[47] This appears to suggest that punitive damages and other forms of noncompensatory damages are not recoverable.

The usual measure of damages in Rule 10b-5 cases is the plaintiff's out-of-pocket loss, which represents the difference between the price the plaintiff paid for the security and the value the plaintiff received for it.[48] There has been some disagreement in court decisions about when the loss should be determined; the majority view on this timing question is that the fair market values of the security and the consideration should be determined as of the date of the fraudulent transaction.[49] An alternative measure of damages, followed in a minority of cases, is a benefit of the bargain measure. This approach focuses on the difference between the value of what the buyer would have received if the fraudulent statements had been true and the value of what the purchaser actually did receive. Beyond these general damage remedies, a successful plaintiff may also recover consequential damages if they can be clearly established by adequate proof.

In some circumstances, however, a defrauded plaintiff may seek a remedy of rescission and not damages. Under this equitable rescission remedy, if successful, the plaintiff will receive back the cost of his or her purchase.[50] The U.S. Supreme Court, in *Randall v. Loftsgaarden*, assumed without deciding that the remedy of rescission was available under section 10(b).[51] If there are supplemental claims under state securities laws, the successful plaintiff may only recover the maximum amount that may be awarded under any single theory of action.[52]

With regard to the federal statute of limitations on federal securities fraud claims, section 804 of the Sarbanes-Oxley Act of 2002 provided a statute of limitations that specified that such a case may be brought no later than (1) two years after the discovery of the facts representing the violation or (2) five years after the occurrence of the violation.

Secondary Liability: Aiding and Abetting Actions for Securities Fraud

An examination of the 1933 and 1934 Acts reveals no mention of secondary liability for aiding and abetting securities fraud. However, primary fraud claims made under the authority of section 10(b) and section 17(a) are occasionally accompanied by claims of secondary liability against parties associated with an allegedly fraudulent transaction. The federal courts have approved of this practice, raising the specter of securities fraud liability for attorneys, accountants, and other transactional advisors.

The legal landscape was significantly altered following the U.S. Supreme Court's 1994 decision in *Central Bank of Denver, N.A. v. First Interstate Bank of Denver, N.A.*, which held that section 10(b) authorized only the SEC and federal prosecutors to bring secondary liability actions, a holding that effectively prohibited private party enforcement. The 1995 Private Securities Litigation Reform Act specifically enabled federal prosecutors and the SEC to bring these section 10(b) actions, continuing the judge-made exclusion of private party enforcement.[53]

The general test for secondary liability under Rule 10b-5 has three components. The enforcing party must prove (1) the existence of a primary violation of securities law; (2) the defendant's knowledge that his or her activity was improper; and (3) that the defendant provided substantial assistance to the primary violation of law. The case law does not present a consistent view of the degree of knowledge necessary for secondary liability. Nonetheless, most courts agree that where there is no duty to disclose, secondary liability should be imposed only when the defendant has actual knowledge of the primary violation and is aware of his or her role in it. As to the third prong of the aiding and abetting test, some courts have held that silence or inaction can constitute substantial assistance while other courts have disagreed.[54] Secondary liability under section 17(a) is far less clear from the case decisions.

Other Sources of Federal Regulation

In the wake of the WPPSS default, the SEC adopted Rule 15c2-12, effective on January 1, 1990, under its 1934 Act anti-fraud authority found in sections 10 and 15B. This was the first SEC action requiring disclosure in the municipal securities business. Rule 15c2-12 regulates underwriter filings and requires disclosures in offerings and sales, to prevent fraud, deception, or manipulation. This rule regulates the behavior of underwriters in relation to the initial offering and sale of municipal securities by regulating the timing and development of disclosure documents. Underwriters must undertake a number of tasks. They are required to obtain and review an official final statement; and prior to making a bid for, or a purchase, offer, or sale of, municipal securities, or a delivery of securities, upon request by a potential customer, they must make available copies of the final official statement for a period of time. This rule applies to primary offerings of municipal securities of $1,000,000 or more, with certain exceptions.

An SEC amendment to the rule in 1995 resulted in a requirement that issuers provide for the filing of annual disclosures. These must supplement and revise the original final official statements with relevant information about post-issuance events. These annual disclosure filings must be provided to each of the municipal securities information repositories recognized by the SEC. The Internet and electronic media have been incorporated into Rule 15c2-12.

Underwriters may use electronic means to distribute disclosures subject to Rule 15c2-12, so long as paper and electronic copies of those disclosures are identical. The MSRB, whose duties are described below more fully, has set up electronic databases to help facilitate the dissemination of disclosed information.

The MSRB

The MSRB was created under the authority of the Securities Act Amendments of 1975, as an independent rulemaking body for the municipal securities industry. Its major purpose is to issue rules governing dealers in municipal securities. While the board's membership is weighted in favor of securities dealers and brokers, the composition of the 15-member board is nonetheless diverse, drawing from the public as well as municipal bond issuers, independent dealers, and bank dealers. These dealers must register with the SEC and comply with the board's rules.

Interestingly, the board operates under the supervision of the SEC, with its rules being subject to SEC approval and amendment. The SEC has concurrent authority with the board; and the SEC, the NASD, and bank regulators have exclusive authority to enforce the board's rules.

Notably, a specific provision in the 1975 law, known as the Tower Amendment, expressly prevents the MSRB from regulating issuers of municipal securities.[55] Therefore, the board's rulemaking authority extends to brokers and dealers of municipal securities but not to the issuers of the securities. This section was intended to assure municipal bond issuers that the regulations governing dealers and brokers would not be passed through to regulate them.

The MSRB has exercised its rulemaking authority, and its rules relate to such diverse topics as professional qualifications, standards of fair practice, recordkeeping, periodic compliance examinations, price quotations of municipal securities, and sales of new issues of securities. These rules carry with them the status of federal law, and they must be observed. A database containing the board's rules, and other regulatory documents, is available on the MSRB's website at www.MSRB.org.

The rules that have been issued by the board fall into three categories:

1. Administrative rules (or "A" Rules A-1 through A-17) relating to the operation and administration of the MSRB
2. Definitional rules (or "D" Rules D-1 through D-12) defining the terms used within the rules themselves
3. General rules ("G" Rules G-1 through G-41) relating to all other matters falling within the board's rulemaking authority

Examples of the MSRB's rules can be found in Rules G-17 through G-41, which are collectively known as the "fair practice rules" and which prohibit brokers and dealers from committing fraudulent or manipulative acts, or engaging in similar behavior. These rules govern a wide range of conduct including advertising (Rule G-21), prices and commissions (Rule G-30), new issue disclosure (Rule G-32), and limits on municipal securities dealers securing business with an issuer within two years after a campaign contribution has been made to an official of the issuer—a practice known as "paying to play" (Rule G-37).

State Regulation of Securities—Blue Sky Laws

Beyond the federal securities laws, many states have passed securities legislation. Some state legislation was even in existence before any federal legislation was first adopted. Kansas was the first state to act, in 1911, with a law that regulated the distribution and sale of securities. These state laws have collectively become known as "blue sky" laws borrowing a phrase from an early U.S. Supreme Court decision, *Hall v. Geiger-Jones Co.*,[56] which described these state laws as being intended to prevent "speculative schemes which have no more basis than so many feet of blue sky." The goal of the state laws is to protect the investing public from fraud and loss from worthless speculative offerings. They typically do require the preparation of a "merit analysis" of investments to determine whether an offering's terms are "fair, just and equitable."

In 1956, the Uniform Securities Act was developed by the National Conference of Commissioners on Uniform State Laws. This model statute, which was substantially updated in 1985, and again in subsequent years, has influenced as many as 39 jurisdictions in the development of their laws. Although state blue sky laws vary, they usually (1) bar fraud in securities transactions; (2) require the registration of brokers and dealers selling securities in the state; and (3) mandate the registration of securities sold within the state. However, state securities laws usually do not regulate securities exchanges, interstate trading, or disclosures by public companies.

With regard to corporate securities, the Uniform Securities Act provides a large degree of uniformity, with a significant number of jurisdictions using the method of registration by coordination for any securities that are registered with the SEC. Interestingly, most states, acting under the Uniform Securities Act, exempt from their own registration requirement securities that are exempt from the federal 1933 Act, including securities such as municipal bonds. On occasion, in order to obtain exemption from state-required registration, states will require that conduit-financing issues comply with state notification or clearance procedures.

Although municipal bond issues may be exempt from state securities registration requirements, in most states, anti-fraud elements of state law do apply. Modeled after federal Rule 10b-5 and section 17(a) of the 1933 Act, section 101 of the Uniform Securities Act makes it unlawful for any person, in connection with the offer, sale, or purchase of any security, directly or indirectly

> (1) to employ any device, scheme, or artifice to defraud,
>
> (2) to make any untrue statement of a material fact or to omit to state a material fact necessary in order to make the statements made, in the light of the circumstances under which they are made, not misleading, or
>
> (3) to engage in any act, practice, or course of business which operates or would operate as a fraud or deceit upon any person.

This section, in conjunction with the provisions of section 410(a)(2) (which is analogous to section 12(2) of the 1933 Act), allows for suit by buyers of all securities (including municipal securities) for recovery of consideration paid for the security plus interest or damages and attorneys' fees.

Following the enactment of the federal Private Securities Litigation Reform Act of 1995,[57] which limited federal court jurisdiction in securities cases, plaintiffs have increasingly sought recovery in state court under state anti-fraud statutes. Congress attempted to rein in this kind of state court litigation with the passage in 1998 of the Securities Litigation Uniform Standards Act[58]—a statute that fundamentally preempts state securities law and forces Rule 10b-5 class actions to be litigated in federal court under federal, not state, law. However, this federal law only applies to "covered securities," a term that does not apply to municipal or state securities. As a result, state securities law remains an effective basis for litigating fraud claims that arise from municipal securities.

Notes

1. 15 U.S.C. § 77a *et seq.*
2. *Id.* § 78a *et seq.*
3. *Id.* § 77C(a)(2).
4. *Id.* § 78c(a)(12).
5. *Id.* § 78aaa *et seq.*
6. *Id.* §§ 77–80.
7. The Public Company Accounting Reform and Investor Protection Act of 2002 is more commonly known as the Sarbanes-Oxley Act after its congressional sponsors.
8. Roger Dunstan, California Research Bureau, Overview of New York City's Fiscal Crisis 7 (1995), *available at* https://www.scribd.com/document/149562131/Overview-of-New-York-City-s-Fiscal-Crisis-1995.
9. Daniel Pope, *A Northwest Distaste for Nuclear Power*, Seattle Times, July 31, 2008, http://seattletimes.nwsource.com/html/opinion/2008082460_nukeop31.html. *See also* SEC, Staff Report on the Investigation in the Matter of Transactions in Washington Public Power Supply System Securities (1988).
10. The MSRB was created by the Securities Acts Amendments of 1975, and its rules are subject to approval by the SEC.
11. These rules, interpretive letters, and interpretive notices may be found on the MSRB website by visiting www.MSRB.org.
12. The Tenth Amendment of the U.S. Constitution reads, "[T]he powers not delegated to the United States by the Constitution, nor prohibited by it to the States, are reserved to the States respectively, or to the people."
13. Nat'l League of Cities v. Usery, 426 U.S. 833 (1976).
14. Maryland v. Wirtz, 392 U.S. 183, 193–99 (1968).
15. Woods v. Homes & Structures of Pittsburg, Kan., Inc., 489 F. Supp. 1270 (D. Kan. 1980).
16. Garcia v. San Antonio Metro. Transit Auth., 469 U.S. 528 (1985).
17. New York v. United States, 505 U.S. 144, 175 (1992).
18. *See* Robert A. Fippinger, The Securities Law of Public Finance (3d ed. 2011).
19. 15 U.S.C. § 77c(a)(2).

20. Landry v. All Am. Assurance Co., 688 F.2d 381, 386 (5th Cir. 1982).
21. Blue Chip Stamps v. Manor Drug Stores, 421 U.S. 723 (1975).
22. Ernst & Ernst v. Hochfelder, 425 U.S. 185 (1976).
23. Aaron v. SEC, 446 U.S. 680 (1980).
24. Osborne v. Mallory, 86 F. Supp. 869, 879 (S.D.N.Y. 1949). *See also Landry*, 688 F.2d at 384 n.10.
25. *See, e.g.*, Bath v. Bushkin, 913 F.2d 817 (10th Cir. 1990); Sears v. Likens, 912 F.2d 889 (7th Cir. 1989); Newcome v. Esrey, 862 F.2d 1099 (4th Cir. 1988) (en banc).
26. Cont'l Bank v. Baker, 777 F. Supp. 92 (D. Mass. 1991).
27. 15 U.S.C. § 77k(c).
28. United States v. Regan, 937 F.2d 823 (2d Cir. 1991).
29. These amendments to the 1934 Act first required registration of municipal securities brokers and dealers, and it resulted in the creation of the MSRB having the authority to regulate brokers and dealers of municipal securities.
30. *In re* Wash. Pub. Power Supply Sys. Sec. Litig., 823 F.2d 1349 (9th Cir. 1987).
31. Sonnenfeld v. City & County of Denver, 110 F.3d 744, 746 (10th Cir. 1996), *cert. denied*, 117 S. Ct. 1819 (1997).
32. Superintendent of Ins. v. Bankers Life & Cas. Co., 404 U.S. 6, 13 n.9 (1971). *See also* Herman & MacLean v. Huddleston, 459 U.S. 375 (1983).
33. Blue Chip Stamps v. Manor Drug Stores, 421 U.S. 723 (1975).
34. Basic Inc. v. Levinson, 485 U.S. 224 (1988).
35. Affiliated Ute Citizens v. United States, 406 U.S. 128, 154 (1972); TSC Indus., Inc. v. Northway, Inc., 426 U.S. 438, 449 (1976); *Basic Inc.*, 485 U.S. 224.
36. Robbins v. Koger Props., 116 F.3d 1441, 1447 (11th Cir. 1997).
37. Ernst & Ernst v. Hochfelder, 425 U.S. 185 (1976).
38. *Id.*
39. *Id.* at 194 n.12.
40. *See, e.g.*, Kennedy v. Tallant, 710 F.2d 711, 720 (11th Cir. 1983); Hackbart v. Holmes, 675 F.2d 1114, 1117 (10th Cir. 1982); Sirota v. Solitron Devices, Inc., 673 F.2d 566 (2d Cir. 1982).
41. Aaron v. SEC, 446 U.S. 680 (1980).
42. Affiliated Ute Citizens v. United States, 406 U.S. 128 (1972).
43. *Id.* at 153–54. The lower federal courts have read a presumption of reliance into the Supreme Court's holding. *See* Lipton v. Documentation, Inc., 734 F.2d 740, 742 n.3 (11th Cir. 1984).
44. *See, e.g.*, Grandon v. Merrill Lynch & Co., 1997 WL 411924 (S.D.N.Y. 1997).
45. *See, e.g.*, Abell v. Potomac Ins. Co., 858 F.2d 1104, 1119 (5th Cir. 1988).
46. Basic Inc. v. Levinson, 485 U.S. 224 (1988).
47. *Affiliated Ute Citizens*, 406 U.S. at 155.
48. Randall v. Loftsgaarden, 478 U.S. 647 (1986).
49. Myzel v. Fields, 386 F.2d 718, 745 (8th Cir. 1967).
50. Quintel Corp., N.V. v. Citibank, N.A., 596 F. Supp. 707, 803 (S.D.N.Y. 1984).
51. *Randall*, 478 U.S. at 666–67.

52. Grogan v. Garner, 806 F.2d 829 (8th Cir. 1986).
53. Private Securities Litigation Reform Act of 1995 § 104.
54. *Compare* Metge v. Baehler, 762 F.2d 621, 625 (8th Cir. 1985), *with* Landy v. FDIC, 486 F.2d 139, 161 (3d Cir. 1973).
55. 15 U.S.C. § 78o-4(d)(1), (2).
56. Hall v. Geiger-Jones Co., 242 U.S. 539 (1917).
57. 15 U.S.C. § 77a *et seq.*
58. *Id.* § 78bb(f)(1) *et seq.*

7

Federal Taxation of Municipal Debt

Introduction

The most common way for localities to supply needed capital facilities, such as buildings, roads, libraries, and other facilities, is to finance them—that is, to borrow the funds needed for their construction and to repay those funds with interest over an extended period. As described in some detail in Chapter 2, local governments have employed a wide variety of financing techniques to meet their capital needs. These include the issuance of general obligation and revenue bonds, lease financing, tax increment financing, bond pools, revolving loan funds, and a host of innovative financing techniques. With all of these financing options, localities have increasingly entered the public capital markets through the issuance of municipal debt securities or bonds. While these government issuers could attempt to finance their needed facilities by competing with nongovernmental borrowers, most choose to avail themselves of a special governmental advantage by issuing bonds whose interest payments are exempt from federal income tax. These tax-free bonds have a significant attraction for persons or entities in high marginal income tax brackets since income derived from them is not federally taxable. As part of the system of fiscal federalism, Congress has chosen this policy of forgoing tax revenue income in combination with grants-in-aid to localities and permitting taxpayers to deduct limited amounts of state and local income and property taxes from the calculation of federal taxable income.

The federal tax exemption feature has a major impact on local governments in that it reduces the cost of obtaining funds for capital projects. In effect, it serves as a federal subsidy for state and local government construction projects and services by reducing interest costs paid on borrowed funds. The exemption also allows local taxpayers to decide which goods and services should be subsidized by the federal government. A comparison of the effective, after-tax income derived from a taxable corporate bond with similar after-tax income from a tax-exempt municipal security demonstrates the extent of this federal subsidy. A taxable corporate bond yielding a 7 percent annual return would provide an investor 4.69 percent in after-tax yield if his or her effective tax rate were 33 percent. One-third of the 7 percent yield would be owed to the federal government as income tax. On the other hand, a tax-exempt municipal bond with similar creditworthiness could pay only 4.69 percent in annual interest to the same owner and it would return the same amount of after-tax income since there would be no federal taxable income represented by the interest paid.[1] Further, if the municipal bond were exempt from state income taxes as well as taxes imposed by the federal government, the interest to be paid to the investor would be even less, since the effective tax-free yield would be the full interest payment received.[2]

In addition to providing a financial advantage to bondholders, the tax-exempt nature of the interest stream from the municipal issuer would also allow the local government to pay for construction of needed facilities at a reduced financing or borrowing cost. In the example above, the interest cost savings to the issuing municipality would be $231,000 on a $10 million bond issue in the first year. To put this advantage in perspective, over the 1980–2007 period, the yield spread between AAA taxable corporate and high-grade tax-exempt bonds ranged from 14 percent to 29 percent,[3] a differential that represents a very significant cost savings to state and local governments.

Not surprisingly, tax-exempt financing has been extremely popular with state and local bond issuers. State and local governments were estimated to have $3.04 trillion in debt as of 2017.[4] At the same time, the impact of tax-exempt financing on federal tax revenues has also been considerable. In 2013, the Internal Revenue Service (IRS) estimated that state and local governments issued $421 billion in tax-exempt bonds.[5] As a result of this expanding state and local government tax-exempt loan debt, the amount of forgone federal income taxes has reached high levels. It has been estimated at $20.5 billion in 2016 and $28.6 billion in 2017. This trend in annual lost federal taxation revenue is projected to continue and grow.

The annual federal revenue loss on tax-exempt bonds was estimated by the Congressional Research Service in 2018 at $422.8 billion from 2017–2026.[6] In fact, the substantial size of this subsidy has provoked serious discussion of the wisdom and efficiency of this federal tax policy. Nonetheless, with limitations that will be discussed below, the federal tax exemption continues in effect for many forms of state and municipal debt.

The Constitutional Basis for Federal Income Tax Exemption

Origins of a Tax Immunity Theory

The issue of whether income derived from state and local government bonds should be subject to federal income taxation has been the subject of a mixture of federal constitutional law and statutory enactments over the period of more than a century. Nothing in the U.S. Constitution explicitly exempts interest on state and local debt from the reach of federal income tax policy. However, in 1895, the U.S. Supreme Court decided *Pollock v. Farmers Loan & Trust Co.*,[7] which identified an exemption grounded in an implied doctrine of intergovernmental immunity supported by the policy basis for the Tenth Amendment. The case arose from a constitutional challenge to an 1894 federal law imposing an income tax without explicitly excluding local government bond interest from the reach of the tax. This early federal income tax law was targeted as an unconstitutional attempt to intrude into state sovereignty. In sweeping language the U.S. Supreme Court found a reciprocal immunity from interference in both the federal and state governments. The *Pollock* opinion held that by taxing state or local bond interest payments received by bond investors, the federal government was imposing "a tax on the power of the states and their instrumentalities to borrow money" and that was "repugnant to the Constitution."[8] The rationale appeared to be that a tax imposed on such a state contract represented a tax on the state government itself. With this holding, the new federal income tax statute was found to be unconstitutional as applied to state and local bond interest. *Pollock*, therefore, stood for the view that the U.S. Constitution barred Congress from passing tax legislation that taxed this kind of income.

In 1913, the 16th Amendment to the U.S. Constitution was ratified. It stated that "Congress shall have power to lay and collect taxes on income, from whatever source derived." Ostensibly, from its literal language, that amendment could have reached state and local interest payments and, by doing so, overrule the *Pollock* decision. Following the passage of the 16th Amendment, academic debate concerning the constitutional basis of municipal bond interest tax immunity raged for decades. Over this same period, the U.S. Supreme Court decided a series of cases that incrementally eroded a constitutional foundation of the immunity doctrine.[9] Nonetheless, all federal income tax statutes enacted since the passage of the 16th Amendment have contained a provision expressly granting an exemption from federal income taxation to interest earned on state and municipal bonds.[10] This statutory pattern reflected a political judgment rather than a constitutional principle.

Moving Away from a Constitutional Basis for Tax Immunity

The trend toward a narrower interpretation of the Tenth Amendment and away from the *Pollock* precedent was announced in the 1985 *Garcia v. San Antonio Metropolitan Transit Authority* case.[11] In *Garcia*, the U.S. Supreme Court overruled its prior decision in *National League of Cities v. Usery*, which had found that federal wage and hour rules violate constitutional principles protecting the states in their "traditional governmental functions."[12] *Garcia* found this test to be unworkable and held that the Tenth Amendment provided the states only "structural" not "substantive" protections. This meant that the states were to look to the national political process, not the federal courts, for protection from excessive congressional interference. *Garcia* effectively limited the judicial role in Tenth Amendment challenges to the reach of federal law.

The final assault on the *Pollock* rule followed the *Garcia* case in the late 1980s after Congress had restricted the federal tax exemption for state and local governmental debt to those bonds that had been issued in registered form, as required by section 310(b)(1) of the 1982 Tax Equity and Fiscal Responsibility Act.[13] Invoking the Supreme Court's original jurisdiction, the State of South Carolina (and intervenors supporting their position) instituted a lawsuit that set out two essential claims. They contended that (1) the Tenth Amendment and constitutional federalism principles and (2) the doctrine of intergovernmental tax immunity required that the U.S. Supreme Court strike down section 310(b)(1) as unconstitutional. After referring the matter to a special master who recommended that the statute be upheld, in a 7–1 decision the Supreme Court rejected both of South Carolina's arguments in *South Carolina v. Baker*.[14] Echoing its *Garcia* holding, the Supreme Court rejected the plaintiff's Tenth Amendment argument based upon its willingness to rely on the national legislative process, concluding that the state governments had not been "commandeered" by the federal government.[15] On South Carolina's second claim of intergovernmental tax immunity, the Supreme Court expressly overruled the *Pollock* ruling, explaining that while relevant in 1895, "[t]he rationale underlying *Pollock* and the general immunity for government contract has been thoroughly repudiated by modern intergovernmental immunity case law."[16] The federal government's taxation of state and local bond interest received by investors is not the same as taxing those governments directly.

The practical effect of the *Baker* holding was to negate, for the most part, the constitutional claim that states were entitled to issue debt whose income was entirely free from federal income taxation. As one commentator has noted, the case "leaves little room for any vestige of a constitutional claim to tax immunity for holders of municipal bonds."[17] However, other constitutional principles, such as the First Amendment's

Establishment Clause, might be argued to limit or bar the use of tax-exempt financing for religious-affiliated institutions.[18] A more recent U.S. Supreme Court decision upheld the common state practice of exempting interest income from bonds and other debt instruments of the state and local governments while taxing interest income arising from bonds of other states and localities. The Court's decision in *Department of Revenue of Kentucky v. Davis*[19] approved of this tax policy against a dormant Commerce Clause challenge, finding the policy to be both necessary and permissible as a competitive borrowing tactic.[20]

In sum, after the *Baker* decision, Congress appears to have broad latitude to adjust or even repeal the statutory tax exemption currently applicable to state and local government bonds. A constitutionally based tax immunity claim seems unlikely to succeed at present. Nonetheless, such a claim might be more successful if a new, highly restrictive federal tax policy has the effect of significantly impeding the ability of states and localities to raise capital for their essential governmental activities. Such a case has not yet arisen.

Practical Significance of Municipal and State Bond Tax Exemption

The main advantage to bond owners of state and local government tax-free bonds is the protection of their interest payments from federal income taxation. More specifically, under the terms of Internal Revenue Code § 103(a), the flow of interest income paid to the owner of a tax-exempt security is excluded from the owner's income when determining gross income for federal income tax purposes. For an individual taxpayer, this means that the taxpayer's gross income, adjusted gross income, and taxable income will all be reduced, usually resulting in a lower tax burden on total income. A corporate taxpayer will experience a similar benefit with a reduction in corporate income that will result in a lessened taxable income. In either case, the actual financial benefit experienced by the taxpayer will depend upon the taxpayer's effective tax rate. The higher the taxpayer's tax rate, the greater the tax savings with tax-free interest.

The appeal of tax-exempt bonds is easily understood by investors in search of a stream of interest payments untouched by federal income taxation. However, these state and local government tax-exempt bonds are not totally free from federal income taxation. Two circumstances exist when federal income tax liability might exist: (1) the sale of state or local government bonds generating a gain or loss[21] and (2) the alternative minimum tax liability when certain bond interest is considered a tax preference item.[22] In the first situation, a municipal bond is considered for federal income tax purposes to be an ordinary capital asset subject to income taxation when there is a gain or loss on its sale. Alternatively, the second example makes the interest paid on most private activity bonds into an item of tax preference that may result in taxing the interest as ordinary income.

The Federal Statutory Tax Exemption: § 103 of the Internal Revenue Code

Basic Statutory Scheme

While other sections of the Internal Revenue Code relate to other features of tax-exempt securities,[23] § 103 is the central provision setting forth the federal income tax exclusion. However, the exclusion does not apply to gains received on the sale or exchange of securities.[24] Section 103(a) establishes that, "except as provided in subsection (b), gross income does not include interest on any State or local bond." This provision is followed by two other subsections, (b) and (c), that (1) create exceptions to subsection (a) and (2) establish basic definitions. The main terms employed by § 103(a) are worthy of special attention.

Bonds as Obligations Bearing Interest

As stated above, § 103(a) excludes from gross income interest earned on "State or local bonds." This category of "State or local bonds" is further defined in § 103(c) to be an "obligation of a State or political subdivision thereof." As straightforward as this statutory language may appear at first glance, there is considerable variation, in practice, with respect to what constitutes an "obligation." Most obviously, an obligation can be a written agreement to borrow money with a scheduled repayment scheme accompanied with the payment of interest. Such an agreement is what most people think of as a municipal bond or debt security; and cases have required that the obligation be incurred by the issuer under a legally valid exercise of its borrowing authority[25] and incurred for a governmental purpose.[26] However, *Drew v. United States* held that this term does not include government installment payments to a property owner of a condemnation award since, in that situation, the debt arose pursuant to the exercise of eminent domain and not municipal borrowing.[27] As noted in Chapter 5, interest paid on municipal obligations may be made out of general tax revenues or out of special funds such as special assessments imposed on landowners who have benefitted from an improvement.[28] Municipal bond interest may be fixed-rate or floating-rate interest paid periodically, or it may be imputed as original issue discount with a growing value that is paid at maturity or sale.[29]

Obligations vary in nature in other ways as well. As discussed in Chapter 5, municipal financing for the acquisition of buildings or equipment may be structured in compliance with state law as a lease rather than a debt transaction. Often this is done to avoid the constraints of state debt limitations. If the transaction has been arranged as a conditional sales contract rather than a lease, the interest payments paid by the government may be considered interest "under an obligation" for federal tax purposes.[30] The same is true for certificates of special assessments for public improvements, which are liens against specific properties where repayment is only from special funds and not general tax revenues.[31] Moreover, for purposes of § 103(a), a range of written agreements that go beyond the conventional debt securities known as municipal bonds may also be deemed obligations.[32]

Proper Issuers of Tax-Exempt Bonds

State or Local Governments and Their Political Subdivisions

As indicated above, under the terms of § 103(a), the federal tax exemption for bond interest only applies to "state or local government bonds." But what issuers of bonds are included within this general category? Section 103(c) adds slightly more detail when it defines this term to mean an "obligation of a State or political subdivision thereof." But what are "political subdivisions" under this important definition? The Treasury regulations issued under this section of the Internal Revenue Code provide a list of potential entities coming within this definition and, not surprisingly, they include the 50 U.S. states and the District of Columbia.[33] Indian tribal governments are treated as states if their bonds are used in the exercise of any "essential governmental function."[34] Similarly, possessions of the United States such as the U.S. Virgin Islands, Puerto Rico, American Samoa, and Guam are also treated as states for purposes of the tax exemption status of their bonds.

While these entities are understandably tax-exempt issuers, the federal tax benefit also extends to their political subdivisions. The term "political subdivision" is more complex than it initially appears. The IRS regulations define a "political subdivision" as "any division of any State or local governmental unit which is a municipal corporation or which has been delegated the right to exercise part of the sovereign power of the unit."[35] An early challenge to a narrow interpretation by the IRS led to the decision in *Commissioner of Internal Revenue v. Shamberg's Estate*, where the Second Circuit ruled that the Port of New York Authority satisfied the requisites for being considered a political subdivision, thereby making their debt interest payments federally tax free.[36] The *Shamberg's Estate* decision identified three sovereign legal powers that were central to the determination of whether an entity is a political subdivision: (1) the power to tax; (2) the power of eminent domain; and (3) the police power. Political subdivisions frequently include special districts established for transportation, utility, or educational purposes.[37]

In subsequent regulations, the IRS has ruled that the body need not necessarily possess all three powers. However, "partial" powers must be significant or substantial in order for "political subdivision" status to be achieved. In *Philadelphia National Bank v. United States*, the Third Circuit ruled that Temple University was not a political subdivision as it possessed limited power in the three areas mentioned above.[38] Revenue rulings have specified the kinds of activities that are eligible for political subdivision status and those that are not. A state university[39] and a multi-district educational association[40] are not considered to be in that desirable category, while a community development authority and a legislatively created regional marketing authority have been included.[41] It is difficult to precisely describe the exact balance of the three sovereign authorities that will be necessary for "political subdivision" status; however, the more of the three categories of general governmental powers that a governmental entity has, the stronger its case will be.

Issuers Acting "On Behalf Of" State or Local Governments

Even if it does not satisfy the tests for "political subdivision" status, an organization may still be able to issue tax-exempt bonds if the entity can be said to be acting "on behalf of" the state or local government. The IRS regulations have recognized an expanded category of tax-exempt issuers that are collectively termed "on behalf of" issuers.[42] There are two subcategories of such issuers: (1) constituted authorities authorized to issue bonds on behalf of political subdivisions and (2) nonprofit entities established under state law complying with Revenue Ruling 63-20 (63-20 Corporations). These two categories of bond issuers are discussed below.

Constituted Authorities. Bonds issued by constituted authorities that are specifically allowed to issue bonds under state law are included within the tax exemption available to state and local governments. The guidelines for this expanded set of debt issuers were set out in Revenue Ruling 57-187,[43] in which the IRS determined that industrial development bonds were to be considered obligations issued "on behalf of a political subdivision" and eligible for tax exemption. Since the issuance of this IRS ruling in 1957, the six criteria it establishes have formed the basis for the legal test for determining whether an entity will be considered a constituted authority empowered to issue tax-free bonds "on behalf of" a state or local government. The relevant criteria may be summarized as follows:

1. The debt issuance must be authorized by a specific state law.
2. The authority must be a public body and its debt must have a public purpose.
3. The governing body of the authority must be under the substantial control of the political subdivision.
4. The authority must have the power to acquire, lease, and sell property and to issue debt to further its purpose.

5. The net earnings of the authority may not inure to the benefit of a private person allowing for the paying of fair value for services rendered to the authority.
6. When dissolved, all of the bond-financed property or assets must vest in the political subdivision creating the authority.[44]

63-20 Corporations. Even if an organization does not satisfy the criteria of Revenue Ruling 57-187, and is thus not recognized as a constituted authority empowered to issue tax-exempt bonds on behalf of a political subdivision, the organization may still be authorized to issue such bonds under certain circumstances. Corporations that are established under general state nonprofit corporation law may issue tax-exempt debt if they comply with the requirements of Revenue Ruling 63-20.[45] These entities are termed "63-20 Corporations," and they are used when state law does not specifically authorize the formation of a public corporation qualifying under Revenue Ruling 57-187, as discussed above. There is, however, a strong similarity between the requirements of Revenue Ruling 63-20 and Revenue Ruling 57-187. 63-20 Corporations must comply with the following five tests in order to be an "on behalf of" debt issuer:

1. The corporation must engage in activities that are public in their nature.
2. The corporation must be one that is not organized as a profit-making enterprise with the exception of retiring its debt.
3. The corporation's net income may not inure to any private person.
4. The state or political subdivision must have a beneficial interest in the corporation and it must have full legal title to the property acquired with the issued debt.
5. The corporation must have been approved by the state or a political subdivision, which must have also approved the specific debts issued by the corporation.

Revenue Procedure 82-26 sets out the circumstances when 63-20 Corporation eligibility will be granted in an advance ruling.[46] Special statutory rules exist for recognizing the debt of a volunteer fire department as tax-exempt debt of the political subdivision;[47] and other statutory sections provide for similar preferential tax-exempt treatment of qualified zone academy bonds and clean renewable energy bonds.

General Rules Applying to All Tax-Exempt Bonds

There are four general rules that apply to all state and local government tax-exempt debt. First, in general, tax-exempt bonds may not be used to reimburse facility capital expenditures that were made more than 60 days prior to the date that a bond issuer adopts a resolution of intent to finance the project with bonds.[48] Presumably, the intent underlying this rule is to encourage expeditious expenditure on project costs and to deter arbitrage. However, there are a few minor exceptions to the prohibition mentioned above. Thus, preliminary expenditures such as architectural, soil testing, or civil engineering fees (ranging up to 20 percent of the bond proceeds), the costs of issuing the bonds themselves, and de minimis amounts may all be reimbursed subject to the IRS regulations.

Second, under Internal Revenue Code § 149(a)(1), tax-exempt bonds that are offered to the general public for a term exceeding one year must be in a book-entry, registered form.[49] Prior to 1983, state and local government bonds had been issued in both registered and bearer forms, with the former requiring a formal listing of ownership and the latter having ownership presumed by possession without such a list. Congress's statutory intent was to prevent income and property from being concealed from the reach of income, estate, and gift taxes.

Third, the Tax Reform Act of 1986 obligates the issuers of all tax-exempt bonds to file reports with the IRS regarding the bonds they have issued.[50] With the increased amount of tax-exempt borrowing occurring at the state and local government levels, the IRS wanted to secure needed information in a regular process and Congress concurred. Municipal bond issuers must now file an IRS report soon after the bond is issued that contains the following information:

1. The name and address of the issuer
2. The date of the issue
3. The amount of the issue's net proceeds
4. The state interest rate, term, and face amount of the issue
5. The issuance costs of the bond issue
6. The amount of reserves maintained for the issue
7. The name of the elected representative who approved the private activity issue or a description of the referendum conducted on the issue

8. The name, address, and employer identification number for each initial principal user, the common parent of a corporate affiliate, and the principal separate issue user, if applicable
9. The certification by the appropriate state official that the issue falls within the state's volume cap
10. Any other information that the IRS may require[51]

Finally, Internal Revenue Code § 149(b)(1) denies federal tax exemption to state and local government bonds whose payment of principal and/or interest is directly or indirectly guaranteed by the federal government. The policy premise behind this restriction is that "where the federal government guarantees or otherwise assures payment, it becomes the effective obligor and the federalism policies of § 103 are not implicated."[52] A federal guarantee may be found directly when either the principal or the interest of bonds is guaranteed by a federal entity. It may also be identified indirectly through investment of bond proceeds in federally insured accounts or otherwise. The 1986 tax legislation went so far as to extend this limit to bonds where only a portion of the debt issue is federally guaranteed.[53] However, exceptions to this restrictive rule do apply to housing-related bonds.[54]

Public Purpose and Private Activity Debt Obligations

Government Purpose Bonds

As noted above, the federal policy premise underlying the exemption from federal taxation of interest income derived from state and municipal bonds is one of federal subsidy for sub-federal governmental operations. Rather than appropriate funds for the construction of fire stations, school buildings, and the like, Congress adopted an income tax statute exempting municipal bond interest from federal income taxation. This policy permitted state and local governments to decide for themselves which governmental facilities were deserving of this attractive federal subsidy.

However, the monetary advantage of this "subsidized" cost of construction financing also appealed to private companies who wished to locate or expand in particular localities. As a result, localities, hoping to support economic development and employment within their borders, often extended the benefits of subsidized construction financing to private companies through the device of industrial development bonds. Employing this technique, a locality could issue tax-exempt debt to finance the development of industrial or other facilities that would then be leased to private firms with the lease payments covering the debt service. Through this approach, bond-financed private plants received an important public subsidy and a significant cost advantage over other private enterprises forced to use conventional financing means.

The industrial development bond method began to encounter resistance from those who believed that it represented a selective and unjustified advantage for certain private projects.[55] Nonetheless, initially the Internal Revenue Code did little to limit the expanding practice of using tax-exempt publicly issued debt. In fact, until the late 1960s, the federal tax code did not specifically prohibit the use of tax-exempt municipal bonds for private purposes. In 1968, however, Congress enacted legislation that barred the issuance of tax-exempt bonds unless the private benefit was small or the use of the proceeds was among those uses favored by Congress.[56] The IRS then followed up this statutory directive by administratively narrowing the acceptable, nongovernmental categories of bond purposes.

Notwithstanding this attempt to restrict the private use of public debt, however, the issuance of this kind of tax-exempt debt skyrocketed. From 1975 through 1985, Congress found that the total volume of private activity bonds grew from $8.9 billion to $116.4 billion, with these bonds representing an ever-increasing proportion of state and local government borrowing.[57] This continuing wide availability of tax-exempt debt for private activities was considered to be "inefficient and disruptive of the equity of the tax system."[58] Critical news stories appeared that described the abuse of the bond tax exemption and emphasized the effect these bonds had in favoring large corporations such as K-Mart and Walmart; and pressure mounted for this form of debt to be further restricted or banned.

Public Purpose and Private Activity Government Bonds

In 1986, Congress finally attempted to respond to the perceived abuses of the federal tax exemption mentioned above. It amended the tax laws by adding § 141[59] and distinguishing between two principal categories of state and local government debt: (1) government bonds and (2) private activity bonds. This dichotomy classified state and local government bonds according to their purposes. More specifically, after 1986, the eligibility of a particular bond for federal tax-exempt status depends upon how the borrowed funds are to be used by the issuing unit. Government or public purpose bonds are typically used for the common functions usually associated with state and local governments, such as the construction of schools, libraries, sewage and water treatment plants, recreation centers, roads and transportation, and a range of other public buildings and facilities. These bonds are generally tax exempt as long as they do not violate the general tax rules and those governing arbitrage.[60]

In contrast, private activity debt generally involves bonds used to finance private, nongovernmental activities. This is true even though the issuer may be a state or local government unit. The rules derived from Internal Revenue Code § 141 are intended to restrict the volume of federally tax-exempt state and local government securities that provide funds for essentially private activities. If a bond is determined to be a private activity bond, the interest it generates will generally be considered federally taxable unless the bond is in one of the designated "qualified" bond categories and it meets other requirements that are described below.[61] In addition, the 1986 tax legislation established a cap or maximum annual amount of qualified private activity bonds for each state through the imposition of a population-related volume ceiling.[62] Up to that maximum amount, the allocation of private activity bonds is allocated by the government of each state. Nonetheless, as discussed below, the scope of § 141 is not entirely clear.

Private Activity Bonds

Section 141 set out the essential ground rules for determining whether a bond is a private activity bond under the Internal Revenue Code. This was a delicate legislative task, since determining the precise boundaries between a public and a private purpose for a bond was considered to be a difficult congressional choice. Section 141(a) establishes an elaborate definition for the key term "private activity bond." The term applies to a debt issue in either of two situations: (1) when it meets the "private business test" of § 141(b) or (2) when it meets the "private loan financing test" of § 141(c). The entire bond issue, not the individual bond, must be evaluated under these tests. Regulations have been developed and issued by the Treasury that help to interpret the statute and to explain which bond issues will be considered private activity bonds.[63] These rules also attempt to identify the situations where the IRS will challenge state and local bonds that violate the letter and the spirit of the 1986 Internal Revenue Code amendments.

Private Business Test

A bond issue may be held to be a private activity bond if it satisfies both components of a two-part "private business test." Unless they independently satisfy the public loan financing test described below, if the bonds only satisfy one of these two elements, they will not be deemed private activity debt and, as a result, they will be considered government bonds eligible for tax exemption. Thus, from the standpoint of the bond issuer, it is usually desirable to "fail" the private business test.

Part one of this test is called the "private business use test." It will be satisfied if more than 10 percent of the bond's proceeds are used (directly or indirectly) in the trade or business of nongovernmental entities.[64] This "use" may be accomplished directly (where proceeds are loaned to a private party) or indirectly (where a municipally bond-financed facility is actually used by a private entity).[65] Use of the bond proceeds by all private entities is added together for federal tax purposes; and the federal government is treated as a private business. A private business use may include any "special legal entitlements to use the financed property under an arrangement with the issuer."[66] The sale or leasing of financed property to a private business would amount to such an entitlement, as would any "management or incentive payment contract."[67] Even more restrictive rules (limited to 5 percent) exist when state or local government bond proceeds are used by a private entity for uses that are "unrelated" to government purposes or "disproportionate" to a government facility also financed by the bond issue.[68] Notably, a facility will not be considered a private activity if it is available for use by the general public.[69] At the same time, use by a private business may be considered use by the general public "only if the property is . . . reasonably available for use on the same basis by natural persons not engaged in a trade or business."[70]

Part two of the private business test, the "private security or payment test," will be met if more than 10 percent of the bond principal or interest will be secured by or derived from payments made with respect to property used in a private business.[71] Such payments make it appear as though the state or local bond was actually used to finance the private business facility.

Private Loan Financing Test

The private loan financing test is the second legal test for determining whether a bond will be considered a private activity bond for federal income tax purposes. This test is met if the bond-issued proceeds that are used (either directly or indirectly) to finance loans to nongovernmental entities exceed the lesser of $5 million or 5 percent of the proceeds of the bond issue.[72] The apparent purpose of this prong of the private activity bond test is to reduce or deter conduit financing practices that would provide publicly raised tax-exempt funds to private users for their own nongovernmental purposes.

Qualified Bonds

If a bond issue is determined to be a private activity bond, its interest will generally be considered federally taxable unless the bonds are for a "qualified" purpose and they meet other general private activity bond rules, as set forth in various sections of the Internal Revenue Code.[73] "Qualified purposes" is a wide-ranging term spanning at least 24 categories of general and specific purposes. Among other things the term includes:

1. *Qualified 501(c)(3) bonds (§ 145)*. These bonds are used by tax-exempt organizations wishing to finance their operations with tax-free debt.
2. *Small issue bonds (up to $10 million) (§ 144(a))*. These bonds are used for manufacturing facilities and first-time farmers.
3. *Exempt facility bonds (§ 142(a))*. Section 142 lists 15 categories of specific bond governmental and nongovernmental uses including airports, docks, commuting and rail facilities, water and sewer facilities, heating and cooling, rental projects, utilities, public education and green buildings, and environmental improvements to hydroelectric plants.

4. *Single-family mortgage revenue bonds (§ 143(a)).*
5. *Veteran mortgage bonds (§ 143(b)).* These provide funds for veterans' residences under specific limits.
6. *Student loan bonds (§ 144(b)).* These provide funds used to make or finance qualified student loans under federal and state programs.
7. *Qualified redevelopment bonds (§ 144(c)).* These provide funds for redevelopment in designated blighted areas.
8. *Enterprise zone facility bonds (§§ 1394 & 1400A).*
9. *New York liberty bonds (§ 1400L(d)).* These provide funds for improving the area of New York City damaged by the September 11th attacks for commercial, residential, and utility purposes.
10. *Gulf opportunity zone bonds (§ 1400N(a)).* These provide tax incentives for the rebuilding of Gulf Coast and hurricane-affected areas.

The broad range of "qualified" bond purposes reflects a congressional preference to provide a subsidy for these specific activities. Despite this, additional restrictions on these qualified bonds are specified in the law.

Volume Cap

In 1986, Congress took important steps to rein in the excessive use of governmental tax-free financing by adopting an annual cap of the volume of most private activity bonds. This cap was expressed in § 146 of the Internal Revenue Code.[74] Beyond defining a maximum annual amount of subsidized debt, the provisions of § 146 demand that each state allocate the volume cap to the most deserving projects in each jurisdiction. In general, a qualified private activity bond must be within a state's volume cap in order for its interest to be tax exempt. However, not all private activity bonds are subject to the volume cap limit.[75]

The total cap ceiling for a state (including state agencies and local governments) was set for 2002 at the larger of $75 per resident or $225 million.[76] The population of any state is derived from the most recent census estimate of the resident population released by the U.S. Census Bureau before the beginning of each calendar year.[77] Adjusted annually for inflation, the cap has risen to $85 per person or more than $256 million for 2007.[78] A state's annual bond volume cap is presumptively split one-half to state government and one-half to local units with the local part allocated according to population.[79] However, the Internal Revenue Code allows state legislatures latitude to alter this allocation;[80] and most state governments have established agencies whose responsibility it is to distribute or allocate the volume cap. Should the cap be exceeded during any year, all bonds issued before exceeding the limit are valid, but those issued thereafter are disqualified from the tax exemption.[81] However, a three-year carry-over provision also exists that allows unused cap volume to be used in subsequent years.[82]

Notably, not all bonds fall under the volume cap. In general, the maximum limit applies to bond issues of qualified redevelopment bonds, qualified student loan bonds, qualified small issue bonds, qualified mortgage bonds, and most exempt facility bonds (except those for airports, docks and wharves, environmental improvements at hydro plants, government solid waste facilities, and high-speed intercity rail facilities), and qualified student loan bonds. However, the same limitation does not apply to qualified § 501(c)(3) bonds, veterans' mortgage bonds, and current refunding bonds.

Percentage Use Requirements

There is a general requirement that 95 percent of the proceeds from exempt facility bonds (net of reserve funds) must be used to provide the specific qualifying facility expenses.[83] The costs of issuing the bonds and working capital are not a qualified cost. However, not more than 2 percent of the face amount of the bond issue may be used for bond issuance expenses. These issuance costs generally include all costs incurred with the debt issue including attorneys' fees, accountants' fees, underwriters' fees and spreads, rating agency fees, and the expense of engineering and feasibility studies.[84] (See Chapters 3 and 4 for more detailed discussion of the bond issuance process.)

Prohibited Facilities Financed with Bond Proceeds

A qualified private activity bond may become disqualified if any part of the proceeds from the issue will be used to finance any of the following facilities: an airplane, a sky box or other private luxury box, health club facilities, gambling facilities, or a retail venue the principal business of which is the sale of alcoholic beverages consumed off premises.[85] These purposes were targeted for exclusion from tax-free status since they were not considered to be deserving of tax-free financing by the IRS and Congress as a matter of policy.

Maturity Rules

Eligible private activity bonds are not deemed a "qualified bond" if the weighted average maturity of the bonds exceeds 120 percent of the average reasonably expected economic life of the facility being financed by the bonds.[86] The intent of this requirement is to avoid the use of tax-free bonds for raising long-term working capital rather than project-specific financing. When the average maturity limits are violated, the sanction is that the bonds will be considered to be federally taxable. Some private activity bonds, however, such as mortgage revenue, veterans' mortgage, and qualified student loan bonds, are not subject to this average maturity requirement.

Land Acquisition and Existing or Used Facilities

No more than 25 percent of the net bond proceeds of an otherwise eligible private activity bond may be used to acquire land or an interest in land.[87] There are exceptions to this percentage limitation for bonds that benefit first-time farmers and for certain other private activity bonds.[88] Moreover, bond proceeds generally may not be used to acquire existing or used property unless the property will be substantially rehabilitated or repaired.[89]

Public Approval Requirements

Over the past 25 years, Congress has become increasingly convinced that the federal tax exemption given to the interest payments on state and local government bonds be allocated only to truly deserving public projects. An additional congressional concern is that certain politically powerful groups be barred from garnering low-interest, federally tax-subsidized loans through favoritism or special influence. As a result, Congress has required public participation in a local government's decision to finance projects with tax-free bonds.

With limited exceptions, private activity bond issues must be approved by the governmental entity issuing the debt as well as by each government with jurisdiction over the land where the new facility is located.[90] The bond issue must be approved after a public hearing preceded by reasonable notice of at least 14 days. The IRS issued "temporary regulations" governing various facets of these hearings prior to the 1986 Tax Reform Act, and it continues to follow them.[91] The required public notice must include a general description of the nature of the facility to be financed and its use, as well as information pertaining to the maximum aggregate face value of the debt, the initial owner, operator, or manager of the project, and the general location of the facility. The intention underlying this notice requirement is to provide the public with sufficient information about the proposed project. Following the hearing, the bond issue may be approved by the elected representatives, or by a public referendum related to a local government financing plan adopted within the prior three years.[92] If the public approval requirement is not satisfied, the bond interest will be considered taxable under federal law.

Post-Issuance Changes in Use

It is important to note that compliance with the numerous rules that apply to qualified private activity bonds will be determined over the entire life or term of the bond issue. Issuers must ensure that their bonds continue to meet the requirements imposed for tax-exempt status even after those bonds are issued. Should a bond issue have a change in use of the bond proceeds or be modified with respect to the bond-financed facilities, its tax-exempt status may be lost.

Rules adopted by the IRS in 1997 apply the private activity bond tests to actual facts as they exist over the entire term of the bond.[93] Qualified private activity bonds may have their tax-exempt status put in jeopardy unless they are eligible for a "remedial action" that is undertaken by the issuer in a timely fashion.[94] The IRS rules provide such remedial actions for qualified § 501(c)(3) bonds, exempt facility bonds, qualified small issue bonds, and redevelopment bonds. It is worth noting that even a government purpose bond may be reclassified and considered a private activity bond with taxable interest payments if the issuer takes "deliberate actions" causing either the private business test or the private loan financing test mentioned above to be satisfied. Moreover, Internal Revenue Code § 150 denies a tax deduction for interest paid to bondholders when a facility financed with private activity debt is not used or owned as required by the regulations.[95]

Arbitrage Bonds

Arbitrage is the practice of buying and later selling the same commodity in different markets having different prices and obtaining a profit by doing so. (This profit is also sometimes referred to as arbitrage.) Arbitrage is a two-step process. In step one, a municipal or state debt issuer sells tax-exempt bonds, paying a relatively low interest rate, and thereby receiving the bond proceeds. In step two, the issuer invests these proceeds in higher-yielding taxable bonds. Under this purchase and sale arrangement, the issuer keeps the "spread" between the interest cost it must pay and the interest payments that it receives; and since the issuer is a state or local government, it will incur no federal tax liability on the interest income earned from its step two investment.

An example may help make the arbitrage transaction understandable. Assume that a municipal issuer sells $100 million in tax-free bonds, paying 4 percent interest, and invests the $100 million of bond proceeds in corporate bonds with a similar term yielding 7 percent interest. The spread (i.e., the difference between the interest cost paid and the interest received) will be 3 percent per year or $3 million. Over a 15-year term, this practice will result in a $45 million arbitrage profit. The municipal issuer will be using its federal tax exemption to "buy" money low and "sell" it high, thereby enjoying investment income from this spread or differential.

This municipal investment strategy was limited by Congress in 1969 when it eliminated the federal tax exemption regarding interest paid on "arbitrage" debt.[96] Later, federal policy regarding municipal arbitrage bonds was concentrated in § 148 of the Internal Revenue Code, as amended by the 1986 Tax Reform Act. The IRS issued detailed regulations in 1993 to implement the statutory framework set forth in § 148.[97] These restrictions, in general, limit the investment return that may be earned with respect to the proceeds of tax-exempt bonds issued by state and local governments. The federal policy on arbitrage bonds seeks to accomplish two goals: restricting the yields that may be earned on tax-exempt proceeds and returning to the federal government any excess earnings made on those proceeds.

The "Reasonable Expectations" Test

An arbitrage bond is defined by § 148(a) as any bond whose proceeds are "reasonably expected (at the time of issuance of the bond) to be used directly or indirectly—1) to acquire higher yielding investments, or 2) to replace funds which were used directly or indirectly to acquire higher yielding investments." The statute further defines "higher yielding investments" as "any investment property which produces a yield over the term of the issue which is *materially higher* than the yield on the issue."[98] Under the IRS "reasonable expectations" test, later events that could not have been anticipated at the time of the bond issuance will not lead to a finding of arbitrage even though the bond issuer actually received a materially higher yield by investing its bond proceeds.

The "reasonable expectations" test focuses on the time of issuance of the bonds. However, the 1986 Internal Revenue Code amendment has been read to cover subsequent intentional acts actually affecting an arbitrage situation.[99] As a result, after municipal bonds are issued, if the issuer intentionally uses any portion of the proceeds of the issue to acquire higher-yielding investments, the bonds will be considered arbitrage bonds and thus taxable, rather than tax-exempt, investments. The 1993 IRS regulations note that if the issuer takes a "deliberate, intentional act" after issuance "in order to earn arbitrage," the bonds will be considered arbitrage bonds if this act had been expected on the issue date.[100] It is sometimes not so clear, however, what intentional acts are intended to earn arbitrage.

Nonarbitrage Certificates

When they close on their debt issue, bond issuers establish the "reasonable expectations" that will establish their compliance with the IRS arbitrage rules by executing a "nonarbitrage certificate." This certificate, which must be formally executed by an official of the issuing entity, sets out the facts and estimates that form the basis of the issuer's expectations. These expectations will establish the basis of bond counsel's opinion that the issue complies with § 148(a). This certificate also usually contains important data needed to determine future compliance with the § 148(f) federal rebate rules. As such, a nonarbitrage certificate must be viewed as an extremely important document for establishing tax compliance.

Computation of the Investment Yield

The determination of whether a municipal bond will be considered an arbitrage bond requires a comparison of the yield on the municipal bond and yield on the investment made with the bond's proceeds. As we have seen, if the yield on the latter investment exceeds that of the municipal bond, arbitrage has resulted. As a general rule, the yield on an investment allocated to a bond issue is based on the discount rate used to determine the present value, on the issue date, of all unconditionally payable receipts to be received from the investment. Payments are the amounts actually or constructively paid to acquire the investment. Payable receipts are the amounts of money actually or constructively received from the investment, including earnings and the return of principal.

Arbitrage Profits: Materially Higher Yields, Temporary Periods, and Reserve or Replacement Funds

Many times, if not most of the time, the money raised by the sale of bonds is quickly spent on construction of a public project and does not result in the acquisition of an investment leading to arbitrage concerns. However, where bond proceeds are invested, they may be held for various "temporary periods" and invested without yield limit during those periods of time.[101] The initial period may last for up to three years,[102] or, in a few categories of long lead time projects, for up to five years.[103] Mortgage and veterans' mortgage bonds have a three-year temporary investment period, while periods of a lesser duration are allowed for revenue anticipation notes and tax anticipation notes, as well as for pooled financing projects.[104] Nonetheless, if the proceeds or funds received from state and local government bond financing are invested during a time outside of the "temporary periods" and earn a higher yield, the practice will be considered arbitrage so long as the differential between the borrowed funds and the investment is "materially higher," a term that IRS regulations define as being more than .125 percent in yield.[105] In other words, where the calculation of investment return exceeds the borrowing cost by .125 percent, arbitrage penalties will apply.

At the same time, though, the law allows for higher reinvestment yields in certain publicly related programs such as student loan funds, or loans to § 501(c)(3) organizations. Similarly, proceeds from qualified mortgage bonds may be lent to homeowners and other borrowers as mortgage loans for a higher yield than is generally allowed with other bonds. Internal Revenue Code § 143(g)(2)(A) provides for a spread of up to 1.125 percent over the cost of raising the funds for these mortgage purposes.[106] The code also imposes certain limits on the use of original bond issue proceeds in a project reserve fund. Generally, no more than 10 percent of an original bond issue may be deposited into such reserve funds unless the IRS specifically determines that more reserves are necessary.[107]

Rebate of Arbitrage Profits

Arbitrage profits must generally be rebated to the federal government every five years, and within 60 days after the retirement of a bond issue. However, there are some exceptions to this general rule that provide protection for governmental bonds, qualified § 501(c)(3) bonds, and small government bond issues of less than $5 million.[108] The IRS has issued complex and detailed regulations governing rebates on arbitrage bonds.[109] These rebate restrictions are significant to bond owners as well as to bond issuers. If rebate rules are violated, previously tax-exempt securities' interest payments will be considered as taxable to the bond owners. Under the terms of § 148, this will be true retroactive to the date of the bond's issuance.[110] At the same time, however, there are certain "reasonable cause" exceptions to this bond owner sanction that may protect bond owners—but not bond issuers—where rebate rules have been infringed.[111]

Notes

1. Grant A. Driessen, Congressional Research Service, Tax-Exempt Bonds: A Description of State and Local Government Debt 2 (2008).
2. If the interest paid to the owner of a bond is exempt from income taxation, the bond is considered to be "tax free." When such interest is not taxable for federal income tax purposes, it is federally tax free. A bond may also be exempt from state and local government income taxation. When this is the case, the bond's income is said to be double or triple tax free.
3. Driessen, *supra* note 1, at 3 tbl. 1.
4. Board of Governors of the Federal Reserve System, Financial Accounts of the United States tbl. D3 (2017).
5. Cynthia Belmonte, *Tax-Exempt Bonds, 2005*, 27 Stat. Income Bull. 156 (2007), *available at* https://www.irs.gov/pub/irs-soi/05govbnd.pdf.
6. Driessen, *supra* note 1, tbl. 2.
7. Pollock v. Farmers Loan & Trust Co., 157 U.S. 429, 583–84 (1895).
8. *Id.* at 586.
9. Metcalf & Eddy v. Mitchell, 269 U.S. 514 (1926) (upholding federal taxes on the income of independent contractors working for a state); Willcuts v. Bunn, 282 U.S. 216 (1931) (allowing the federal taxing of capital gains resulting from the sale of municipal debt); Helvering v. Gerhardt, 304 U.S. 405 (1938) (upholding federal tax on the income of public authority employees); Graves v. New York *ex rel.* O'Keefe, 306 U.S. 466 (1939) (allowing a state to tax the income of an employee of a federal entity).
10. Internal Revenue Code § 103 provides the most recent example of this exemption.
11. Garcia v. San Antonio Metro. Transit Auth., 469 U.S. 528 (1985).
12. Nat'l League of Cities v. Usery, 426 U.S. 833, 840 (1976).
13. 26 U.S.C. § 149(a).
14. South Carolina v. Baker, 485 U.S. 505, 526–27 (1988).
15. *Id.* at 513, 515.
16. *Id.* at 520.
17. Robert S. Amdursky & Clayton P. Gillette, Municipal Debt Finance Law: Theory and Practice 444 (1992).
18. *See* Hunt v. McNair, 413 U.S. 734 (1973); Mitchell v. Helms, 530 U.S. 793 (2000); Zelman v. Simmons-Harris, 536 U.S. 639 (2002).
19. Dep't of Revenue of Ky. v. Davis, 128 S. Ct. 1801 (2008).
20. *Id.* at 1812.
21. Willcuts v. Bunn, 282 U.S. 216, 232 (1931).
22. I.R.C. § 57(a)(5).
23. *Id.* §§ 141–150. The rules applying to private activity bonds are found in §§ 142 through 147 and § 149, while the rules defining arbitrage bond policy are found in § 148.
24. *Willcuts*, 282 U.S. at 232.
25. The obligations must be valid under the substantive and procedural requirements of state law. *See* Rev. Rul. 87-116. *See* Power Equip. Co. v. United States, 748 F.2d

1130 (6th Cir. 1984) (holding that debt incurred invalidly under state law is not an "obligation" under § 103(a)).
26. U.S. Trust Co. of N.Y. v. Anderson, 65 F.2d 575 (2d Cir. 1933); Newlin Mach. Corp. v. Comm'r, 28 T.C. 837 (1957); Drew v. United States, 551 F.2d 85 (5th Cir. 1977).
27. *Drew*, 551 F.2d 85.
28. *See* Rev. Rul. 54-106.
29. I.R.C. § 1271-75.
30. *See* Rev. Rul. 55-540.
31. Indep. Gravel Co. v. Comm'r, 56 T.C. 698 (1971).
32. King's County Dev. Co. v. Comm'r, 93 F.2d 33 (9th Cir. 1937).
33. I.R.C. § 103(c)(2). *See also* Treas. Reg. § 1.103-1.
34. I.R.C. § 7871(a)(4), (c)(1). Tribal governments may issue tax-exempt private activity bonds for manufacturing facilities as an exception to the general ineligibility of private activity bonds for federal tax exemption. *Id.* § 7871(c)(3).
35. Treas. Reg. § 1.103-1(b).
36. Comm'r of Internal Revenue v. Shamberg's Estate, 144 F.2d 998 (2d Cir. 1944), *cert. denied*, 323 U.S. 792 (1945).
37. Treas. Reg. § 1.103-1(b).
38. Phila. Nat'l Bank v. United States, 666 F.2d 834 (3d Cir. 1981).
39. Rev. Rul. 77-165, 1977 WL 43881 (1977).
40. Tex. Learning Tech. Group v. Comm'r of Internal Revenue, 958 F.2d 122 (5th Cir. 1992).
41. Rev. Rul. 1955-1 C.B. 14, 1955 WL 9538 (1955).
42. Treas. Reg. § 1.103-1(b).
43. Rev. Rul. 57-187, 1957-1 C.B. 65.
44. *Id.*
45. Rev. Rul. 63-20, 1963-1 C.B. 24.
46. Rev. Proc. 82-26, 1982-1 C.B. 476.
47. I.R.C. § 150(e)(1)(A).
48. Treas. Reg. § 1.150-2.
49. *Id.* § 5f.103-1(c)(1).
50. I.R.C. § 149(e)(2).
51. *Id.*; Treas. Reg. § 1.149(e)-1; Treas. Reg. § 5f.103-3.
52. AMDURSKY & GILLETTE, *supra* note 17, at 460.
53. I.R.C. § 149(b)(2).
54. *Id.* § 149(b)(3)(A).
55. Hart H. Spiegel, *Financing Private Ventures with Tax-Exempt Bonds: A Developing "Truckhole" in the Tax Law*, 17 STAN. L. REV. 224 (1965).
56. C. Willis Ritter, *Federal Income Tax Treatment of Municipal Obligations: Industrial Development Bonds*, 25 TAX LAW. 511, 513 (1972).
57. STAFF OF JOINT COMM. ON TAX'N, 99TH CONG., GENERAL EXPLANATION OF THE TAX REFORM ACT OF 1986, at 1151 (Comm. Print 1987) (by 1985, 53 percent of state and local debt was for private activities).
58. BORIS I. BITTKER & LAWRENCE LOKKEN, FEDERAL TAXATION OF INCOME, ESTATES, AND GIFTS § 15.2 (2008).

59. I.R.C. § 141.
60. Arbitrage limitations have been established in the statutory and administrative provisions governing tax-exempt debt. The essential policy objective of these limits has been to reduce or eliminate the use of the federal tax exemption as a means of obtaining investment income for state and local bond issuers.
61. I.R.C. § 141(e)(1)(A)–(G).
62. *Id.* § 146.
63. Treas. Reg. §§ 1.141-1 to 1.141-16.
64. I.R.C. § 141(b)(1), (6).
65. Treas. Reg. § 1.103-7(b)(3).
66. *Id.* § 1.141-3(b)(1).
67. *Id.* § 1.141-3(b)(2), (b)(3).
68. I.R.C. § 141(b)(3)(A), (B).
69. *Id.* § 141(b)(6)(A). *See also* Treas. Reg. § 1.141-3(c); rules for use of "output facilities" or public utilities that are generally used by the public.
70. Treas. Reg. § 1.141-3(c)(1).
71. I.R.C. § 141(b)(2)(B).
72. *Id.* § 141(c).
73. *Id.* § 103(a), (b)(1).
74. *Id.* § 146.
75. *See id.* § 146(g), (h) & (i).
76. *Id.* § 146(d)(1).
77. *Id.* § 146(j).
78. Rev. Proc. 2006-53, 2006-48 I.R.B. 996, § 3.16.
79. I.R.C. § 146(c)(1).
80. *Id.* § 146(e)(1), (3) (exception for constitutional home rule cities).
81. *Id.* § 146(a).
82. *Id.* § 146(f)(3)(A).
83. *Id.* § 150(a)(3).
84. *Id.* § 147(g)(1). If the 2 percent limit will be exceeded, then these costs must be paid from non–bond proceed sources.
85. *Id.* § 147(e).
86. *Id.* § 147(h)(1).
87. *Id.* § 147(c)(1)(A).
88. *Id.* § 147(h)(1)–(3) (mortgage revenue, veterans' mortgage, student loan, § 501(c)(3), and public-private school bonds).
89. *Id.* § 147(d)(1) (exception for rehabilitation expenses).
90. *Id.* § 147(f) (refunding, airport, and high-speed intercity rail projects excluded).
91. Treas. Reg. § 5f.103-2.
92. I.R.C. § 147(f)(2)(B), (C).
93. Treas. Reg. § 1.141-2(d)(1).
94. *Id.* §§ 1.141-12, 1.142-2, 1.144-2, 1.145-2, 1.147-2.
95. I.R.C. § 150(b).
96. *Id.* § 103(c)(2).

97. Treas. Reg. §§ 1.148-0 to 1.150-1.
98. I.R.C. § 148(b)(1) (emphasis added).
99. Treas. Reg. § 1.148-2(b).
100. *Id.* § 1.148-2(c).
101. *Id.* § 1.148-2(c)(2)(i)(A)–(C) (the expenditure test, the time test, and the due diligence test).
102. *Id.* § 1.148-2(e)(2)(i).
103. *Id.* § 1.148-2(e)(2)(ii).
104. *Id.* § 1.148-2(e)(3), (4).
105. *Id.* § 1.148-2(d)(2)(i).
106. I.R.C. § 143(g)(2)(A).
107. *Id.* § 148(d)(2).
108. *Id.* § 148(f)(4)(B)(i), (ii).
109. Treas. Reg. § 1.148-3 (general arbitrage bond rules).
110. I.R.C. § 148(f)(1).
111. *Id.* § 148(f)(7)(C).

8

Issues and Procedures in Municipal Finance Litigation

INTRODUCTION

Carefully prepared, adequately supported, and well-structured municipal bonds rarely result in litigation. Nonetheless, lawsuits can and do result from the issuance of municipal securities, particularly where governmental entities are embroiled in fiscal crises, and a bond default occurs or the possibility of one looms. Municipal attorneys must be prepared for the possibility of such disputes, and they must defend their client with vigor and skill where they arise. Similarly, attorneys for bondholders must be aware of their clients' rights, and ready and able to pursue legal action where doing so will advance their clients' interests.

This chapter considers the issues that typically arise in municipal bond litigation. It begins with an overview of the types of actions that may be brought with respect to municipal financial instruments. It then surveys the procedural issues that generally arise where such actions are initiated. In particular, the chapter focuses on questions of jurisdiction and such related matters as venue and justiciability. It also considers pertinent issues involving pleadings, motion practice, class actions, discovery, trial, and remedies in municipal bond lawsuits.[1]

Legal Bases for Municipal Bond Lawsuits

Bond litigation most typically arises in circumstances where bond-issuing municipalities are faced with significant cash flow difficulties, and financial crises result. Such problems may stem from one or a multitude of causes. Changes in general economic conditions, such as depressions, recessions, or rapid increases in interest rates, are often to blame. So too is the misguided use of bond financing for projects that turn out to be unnecessary or infeasible, incompetent municipal management, fraud and theft, the impact of natural disasters, and the simple unwillingness of municipal officials to make good on their debts. Fortunately, whatever their cause(s) may be, municipal bond defaults are relatively rare occurrences. Since 1839, local governments in the United States have defaulted on municipal bonds fewer than 10,000 times. Nearly 50 percent of those defaults took place during the Great Depression (from 1929 to 1937). In those difficult years, local governments defaulted on the payment of interest and principal on approximately 18 percent of the total amount of municipal bonds outstanding. Since the 1930s, however, the incidence and volume of bond defaults declined precipitously. Thus, from 1945 to 1970, only 0.4 percent of the principal amounts of bonds outstanding went into default, a trend that has continued thereafter.[2]

Notwithstanding their relative rarity, however, when they do occur, municipal bond defaults frequently roil credit markets, do grave damage to state and municipal creditworthiness, and result in the potential for serious monetary losses to bondholders. In such circumstances, the lawsuits that result are of two general types: actions for damages—usually under color of federal securities laws or the Racketeer Influenced and Corrupt Organizations Act (RICO)—and lawsuits aimed at determining the validity or enforceability of the municipal bond issuer's obligations.

Under the Securities Act of 1933, primary offerings of municipal securities were not subjected to the registration requirements that apply to corporate securities.[3] Similarly, as discussed in Chapter 6 at greater length, municipal bonds were defined as "exempted securities," and thus made exempt from the reporting requirements of the Securities Exchange Act of 1934.[4] Nonetheless, in the wake of the New York City financial crisis of the 1970s, Congress enacted the Securities Acts Amendments of 1975, legislation that created a significantly new regulatory structure for municipal securities dealers.[5] Although the 1975 amendments did not repeal the exemption of municipal securities from federal securities laws, it made the anti-fraud provisions of the Securities Exchange Act, including the prohibition on insider trading of U.S. Securities and Exchange Commission (SEC) Rule 10b-5, applicable to municipal issuers of bonds.[6] In addition, the amendments established a new Municipal Securities Rulemaking Board with the authority to adopt rules governing transactions conducted by dealers in municipal securities.[7]

Where bondholders bring action to recover money damages, they frequently rely on the applicable federal securities laws to recover their monetary losses from a bond-issuing municipality (and other parties) under theories of common law fraud or breach of fiduciary obligation. Such plaintiffs may also rely upon the bond instrument itself in an action against the municipal obligor that amounts, in essence, to a lawsuit for breach of contract. Additionally, bondholders may bring lawsuits to obtain a judicial determination as to the validity of existing or proposed municipal obligations. The most common action of this type is a suit in federal court for a declaratory judgment (i.e., a judicial declaration of the rights and obligations of the parties to a concrete dispute). Such a declaration can validate or invalidate a municipal securities issue, either before or after it is sold to the public. Where a declaratory judgment is sought *prior to* the sale of bonds, that request is typically combined with a request for an injunction against the issuance or sale of the instruments. On the other hand, where a declaratory judgment is requested *following* a bond sale, an injunction against the use of the proceeds is often demanded.

In a minority of states, special procedures have been established by legislation under which the validity of municipal securities may be adjudicated in state court prior to their issuance. The particular procedures for obtaining a validation judgment vary from state to state. In a few jurisdictions, only the state is entitled to initiate a validation proceeding. In other states, however, many more parties—including taxpayers and property owners as well as bond-issuing local governments—may seek validation judgments. Once issued by courts, validation decrees are generally binding upon all persons, even those who were not parties to the proceeding. By assuring potential purchasers that the validity of the securities covered by the decree will not be subject to further legal challenge, validation decrees thus serve to enhance investor confidence in those bonds.

Jurisdictional Issues

Municipal securities–related lawsuits brought in the federal courts must satisfy the federal requirements that pertain to both subject matter and personal jurisdiction. Subject matter jurisdiction may be premised on the existence of a "federal question," diversity of citizenship among the parties, or "supplemental jurisdiction" over state claims that are closely related to claims in the action within the court's original jurisdiction. If the federal court does not have subject matter jurisdiction, the lawsuit in question will be dismissed, either upon the motion of a party or by the court sua sponte; and dismissal for lack of subject matter jurisdiction may occur at any time, even after judgment has been entered in the suit.[8]

Without regard to the amount in controversy, the federal courts have general jurisdiction over actions arising under the Constitution and laws of the United States.[9] It is therefore clear that municipal securities lawsuits involving claims of fraud under the federal securities laws are within federal jurisdiction. In contrast, actions that raise only questions of state statutory or common law are clearly not within federal question jurisdiction. For that reason, unless there is diversity of citizenship or some basis exists for supplemental jurisdiction, issues concerning a municipality's legal authority to issue bonds as well as matters involving the interpretation of bonds (or contracts for the payment of bond proceeds) are generally litigated in state courts. The federal courts also have subject matter jurisdiction as to actions between citizens of different states in which the amount in controversy exceeds $75,000.[10] By well-established case law, citizenship is determined at the time the action is commenced, as opposed to the time that the claim arose.[11] Moreover, diversity must be complete, in the sense that all of the plaintiffs must be citizens of states different from those of all of the defendants.[12]

In municipal securities litigation, the amount in controversy is generally viewed as the value of the bond issue that is the subject of the suit. Municipal corporations, like most political subdivisions of a state, are deemed to be citizens of the state in which they are incorporated.[13] And for purposes of diversity of citizenship, banks, trust companies, and other corporations are considered citizens of both the state in which they have their principal place of business and the state in which they are incorporated.[14] One question that sometimes arises in municipal finance suits is whether a trustee who sues on behalf of a group of bondholders should be considered a citizen of the state in which the bondholders reside or a citizen of the state in which the trustee is a resident. To decide that question, the courts have tended to focus on whether the trustee is merely a nominal, passive holder or whether he or she is authorized to exercise power on the bondholders' behalf in a more active manner. The residence of the bondholders controls in the former situation, while the trustee's state of residence is paramount under the latter circumstances.[15]

Where plaintiffs in municipal bond cases have claims that arise under both federal and state law (e.g., where holders of defaulted bonds assert causes of action for securities fraud and also seek recovery for negligent misrepresentation and common law fraud), the federal courts may have supplemental subject matter jurisdiction to hear the entire case. The Federal Judicial Code grants such jurisdiction as to state law claims that form part of "the same case or controversy under Article 3 of the United States Constitution."[16] For supplemental jurisdiction to exist, three conditions must be satisfied: (1) there must be original federal subject matter jurisdiction over at least one of the plaintiff's claims; (2) both the federal and the state claims must arise out of the same "nucleus of common fact"; and (3) all of the claims must be sufficiently related that they would ordinarily be tried together in a single proceeding.[17] The granting of supplementary jurisdiction is discretionary. The code sets out four situations in which federal district courts may decline to exercise it: (1) the claim raises a novel or complex issue of state law; (2) the state law–based claim "substantially predominates" over the plaintiff's federal law claim; (3) the district court has previously dismissed the plaintiff's federal claims; and/or (4) there are other, compelling reasons for the court to decline jurisdiction.[18] In municipal securities cases, federal courts typically grant subject matter jurisdiction as to state law claims that relate to claims based upon federal securities laws or the federal RICO statute.[19] The same thing is generally true where the district court's jurisdiction is founded on diversity of citizenship. In the latter class of actions, however, there can be no supplemental jurisdiction over state law claims that plaintiffs make against third-party defendants, third-party counterclaim defendants, permissibly joined parties, or indispensable parties, where the exercise of that supplemental jurisdiction would be inconsistent with generally applicable diversity jurisdiction requirements.[20]

In contrast with subject matter jurisdiction, personal jurisdiction is the power of a court to make legally valid decrees with respect to particular legal entities, such as municipalities, corporations, and individuals. In both federal and state courts, personal jurisdiction questions implicate the Due Process Clauses of the Fifth and 14th Amendments to the U.S. Constitution, since those constitutional provisions have been construed to require that the courts exercise jurisdiction over persons only when a defendant has been given notice of the proceeding and an opportunity to be heard.[21] These issues can be quite significant in municipal bond litigation, which often involves a multitude of parties, not all of whom will be amenable to suit in all jurisdictions. As a general matter, in applying the Due Process Clauses, courts will ask whether a party may be hauled into court in a distant forum consistent with traditional notions of "fair play and substantial justice." To resolve that question, the courts have evolved a "minimum contacts test." This judicial formula focuses on whether—taking account of the relationship among the defendant, the forum, the lawsuit, the federal interest in efficient resolution of controversies, and the interests of the states in their own social policies—the defendant has had sufficient minimum contacts with the forum in question that the exercise of personal jurisdiction over the defendant is reasonable.[22] Where litigation concerns the validity of bonds and the liability of their municipal issuers, personal jurisdiction over the issuing entity as well as bondholders and others summoned in connection with the suit may generally be established in the forum where the municipal bond issuer is located. Moreover, municipal officials, bondholders, accountants, and other parties may typically be subject to personal jurisdiction in the bond issuer's forum, or in any other forum to which those parties have travelled to conduct negotiations or to perform or participate in activities called for in a bond-related contract.[23]

In federal court actions where the court's subject matter jurisdiction is based upon a federal question, personal jurisdiction is governed by federal principles. In municipal securities actions based upon federal securities laws and federal racketeering statutes, the statutes themselves authorize the federal courts to exercise nationwide service of process.[24] Where no federal statute contains such an express authorization, however, personal jurisdiction may be established under the Federal Rules, consistent with due process requirements, by service of a summons or by the filing of a waiver of service.[25] On the other hand, where a federal court's basis for subject matter jurisdiction is diversity of citizenship, or the action is brought in a state court, personal jurisdiction over the defendant must be based on the state's "long-arm statutes." Long-arm statutes differ in their particulars. However, most of them require that a defendant "do business" in the jurisdiction, or commit a tort or contract to supply goods or services in the state, and/or there must be a "nexus" between a plaintiff's cause of the action and the transaction of some business in the state by the defendant. In fact, in municipal securities cases of this kind, long-arm statutes do generally provide a basis for personal jurisdiction over most potential defendants in the state or federal district where the municipality is located. Many of the potential defendants in such matters will have previously conducted activities or performed services in that jurisdiction. Personal jurisdiction over them may thus be obtained there.

Venue

In the federal courts, venue is governed by a statute that provides that in civil suits, where jurisdiction is based solely on diversity of citizenship, the action may be brought only in the judicial district in which all of the plaintiffs reside or in which the claim arose.[26] Civil actions not founded on diversity may only be brought in the federal district where all of the defendants reside or in which the claim arose.[27] For purposes of venue, corporations (including municipal corporations) are deemed to reside in any judicial district in which, at the commencement of the lawsuit, they are subject to personal jurisdiction;[28] and where public officials are sued in their official capacities, they are viewed as residents of the place in which they perform their official duties.[29] In municipal securities litigation that is based upon federal securities laws, venue may be proper in *any* district in which the defendant performed an act that contributed to a scheme to defraud.[30] This may be a district in which the offer or sale of the instrument occurred, or a district in which the defendant is found, is an inhabitant, and/or conducts business.[31]

Parties who are dissatisfied with the plaintiff's choice of forum may move to dismiss on the ground of forum non conveniens.[32] The gist of such a motion is that the chosen forum is substantially less convenient than another forum. In the federal courts, if such a motion is granted it generally results in a transfer of the lawsuit to a district where the action might have initially been brought, where trial of the suit is more convenient to the parties and witnesses, and where (in the court's judgment) the interests of justice will be better served.[33] Where multiple districts are involved, the decision as to where to transfer the action, for purposes of pretrial proceedings, will be made by a "judicial panel on multi district litigation" authorized by statute.[34] This panel usually gives considerable weight to the extent to which pretrial proceedings have advanced in the potential transferee districts, and to which judge is most familiar with the facts and legal issues.[35]

Venue is also sometimes an issue in municipal bond lawsuits brought in the state courts. Many state venue statutes provide that venue must be brought in a county where one of the parties resides or does business, or where the property in question is located. Where a municipal corporation is involved, venue will generally lie in the county or district where that municipal corporation is located. Conflicts arise, however, where more than one municipality is involved in the litigation. In those instances, state courts, like their federal judicial counterparts, will balance the convenience of the parties and witnesses, and consider the interests of justice, in applying a forum non conveniens analysis to determine where the case will be heard.

Justiciability and Related Questions

In the federal courts, justiciability encompasses a live "case or controversy," whether the case is ripe for decision, whether the matter is moot, and whether the plaintiff has standing to sue. Moreover, even where a case satisfies all applicable justiciability requirements, it may still be dismissed on the basis that there is a conflict between a federal and a state court that makes it appropriate for the court to "abstain" from exercising its decisional power. Article III, section 2 of the U.S. Constitution limits the jurisdiction of federal courts to actual, concrete cases or controversies. Courts are not empowered to hear hypothetical cases, feigned or collusive cases, or cases in which an advisory opinion is sought.

The case or controversy requirement sometimes plays a role in bond-related lawsuits. Thus, for example, it has been held that state validation proceedings may not be removed to federal courts because they improperly seek an advisory opinion.[36] A case or controversy question also arose where trustees of securities were in the dark as to whether a bond issuer had defaulted on its bonds, and thus in doubt as to whether to declare a default—which might throw the issuer into bankruptcy—or to do nothing and risk violating a fiduciary duty to their investors if a default had occurred. On those facts, the trustees were denied a declaratory judgment on the ground that their lawsuit was effectively a request for an advisory opinion.[37]

Questions of ripeness are also sometimes raised in bond litigation. Ripeness refers to a situation where a case has arrived at the point that the facts are sufficiently developed that a court may usefully and intelligently adjudicate the matter. In the federal system, cases must present a controversy of "sufficient immediacy and reality" that the issuance of a judgment is warranted.[38] In the context of municipal securities lawsuits, ripeness questions are most likely to arise in actions that seek to enjoin municipalities from issuing bonds. In such matters, the courts have found the case to be ripe when there is a real possibility that the defendants will issue the controverted bonds, as opposed to a mere speculative possibility of such action.[39] Also, in at least one case, a federal court dismissed, on ripeness grounds, a city's attempt to enjoin the commencement of a formal SEC investigation into its municipal securities where the SEC had provided assurances that it had made no decision as to whether it would actually conduct such an investigation.[40]

The basic notion of the doctrine of mootness is that a court will not entertain a case when the plaintiff no longer has a personal stake in the outcome of the litigation. In municipal bond cases, the question of mootness may arise where a plaintiff bondholder has sold a bond prior to bringing suit. In such instances, the action will be moot unless the plaintiff can demonstrate that the actions of the defendant caused the value of his or her instrument to decrease. Mootness may also be raised as a defense in a municipal securities class action where the named plaintiff no longer has a stake in the dispute. In cases of that sort, it has been held that even though the named plaintiff's claim must be dismissed on mootness grounds, the remaining class members may continue to pursue their claim so long as they have been certified as a class and their interest in the action remains active and ongoing.[41]

The standing-to-sue requirement is intended to ensure that the parties to a lawsuit are genuine adversaries who will pursue their interests throughout the litigation vigorously and without collusion. To have standing, a plaintiff must generally show that he or she has suffered (or is threatened with) a "distinct and palpable injury" that is fairly traceable to the defendant's conduct, and that can be redressed by the relief requested.[42] As a general matter, parties who are affected financially by actual or threatened municipal bond defaults—including bondholders, bond trustees, municipalities, and municipal officials—will have standing to bring action to recover or prevent their monetary losses. Moreover, at least in some jurisdictions, in appropriate cases, taxpayers and ratepayers also have standing to sue. State laws vary in the extent to which they confer standing to sue upon taxpayers. Where they do have standing, taxpayers must typically demonstrate that they have an individual interest that is different from that suffered by the general public,[43] or that they are alleging a specific injury beyond a mere increase in tax rates.[44] In other states, taxpayers are granted the right to bring a "derivative action" on behalf of a local governmental entity in pursuit of a claim based upon an injury to the local government, as opposed to the taxpayer himself or herself.[45]

The doctrine of abstention holds that federal courts may abstain from exercising their judicial authority in cases where there may be a conflict between federal and state courts. It is based upon notions of comity and federal judicial respect for the autonomy of states and their lawmaking powers. Abstention is applied in cases involving constitutional challenges to state actions where there are unsettled questions of state law.[46] Federal courts will also abstain from deciding cases that would interfere with state administrative proceedings where the exercise of federal jurisdiction would disrupt state efforts to establish a coherent policy on a matter of substantial public concern,[47] and where a state criminal prosecution is challenged in federal court.[48] Abstention issues arise in municipal bond litigation from time to time. Relying on abstention, federal courts have declined to adjudicate claims for payment on bonds where the issue of whether the bonds were enforceable is still pending in the state courts.[49] In other cases, however, federal courts have declined abstention and gone ahead to decide bond-related disputes. That has been done in situations where state courts had already adjudicated the pertinent legal questions,[50] where there were no unsettled questions of state law,[51] where there was no opportunity for state judicial review of the issues raised,[52] and where there was no pending state proceeding.[53]

Pleading

In the federal courts, complaints are required to include allegations that "plausibly suggest a cause of action,"[54] and the same pleading approach is applicable to other pleadings, including answers, counterclaims, and replies. Moreover, in the absence of bad faith, the courts will freely allow parties leave to amend their pleadings without prejudice.[55] Notably, however, different pleading rules apply with respect to actions based upon theories of fraud, including bond-related lawsuits premised on the anti-fraud provisions of federal securities legislation and/or RICO.[56] In such actions, under Rule 9(b) of the Federal Rules of Civil Procedure and a host of similar state procedural requirements, fraud or mistake must be pleaded with particularity. This rule is intended to prevent the filing of complaints simply as a way of discovering unknown wrongs. It also has the purpose of allowing full notice to a party charged with fraud, and giving that party a complete opportunity to defend the lawsuit as well as his or her reputation.[57]

The Private Securities Litigation Reform Act of 1995 (Reform Act) provides that a plaintiff in a federal securities fraud action must set forth specifically in his or her complaints each statement of the defendant that is alleged to have been misleading, the reasons it was misleading, and (where required) the facts giving rise to "a strong inference that the defendant acted with the required state of mind."[58] In fact, the federal courts vary a good deal in the approaches they take to the "required state of mind" in such lawsuits.[59] However, there is general agreement that circumstantial evidence may be used to show how and why a defendant's statements were misleading.[60] Moreover, it is well settled that the plaintiff must show that his or her economic losses were a result of the defendant's misrepresentations or omissions by demonstrating that those losses were a foreseeable consequence of the defendant's statements.[61]

Motion Practice

When a motion to dismiss is before a court, it is axiomatic that the court must accept the plaintiff's well-pleaded allegations as true, and all reasonable inferences of fact must be drawn in the plaintiff's favor. In municipal securities actions, that principle requires the courts to accept as true the plaintiff's interpretation of financial documents unless the plaintiff's interpretation is totally without a factual basis.[62] Well-pleaded complaints in municipal bond litigation are generally not dismissed. Nonetheless, in lawsuits relating to bonds, a motion to dismiss may be granted on one or more of a number of grounds, including (among others) the expiration of a statute of limitations, a plaintiff's failure to plead fraud with particularity, sovereign immunity, abstention, nonjusticiability, designation of an incorrect municipal official as a defendant, and res judicata. In addition, under the Reform Act, a defendant may successfully have an action for securities fraud dismissed where that party's allegedly misleading statement was a "forward looking statement" (i.e., a statement of future plans or a projection of financial results that contains a statement describing factors that may cause actual results to differ from those that have been predicted).[63]

When there is no genuine issue of material fact, and the plaintiff is entitled to judgment as a matter of law, the plaintiff is entitled to have a court grant a motion for summary judgment in its favor. Such a motion presents the question of whether there are "genuine issues," a phrase that has been construed to refer to issues involving evidence that would provide a sufficient basis for a trier of fact to return a verdict in favor of the nonmoving party.[64] Similarly, a "material fact" is a fact that is susceptible of altering the outcome of the litigation.[65] In the federal courts, the court is authorized to grant summary judgment with regard to all or only part of a party's claim,[66] and if practicable the court must grant partial summary judgment as to questions not in dispute to narrow the factual issues to be determined at trial.[67] In municipal bond lawsuits based upon fraud, the question of whether a defendant has committed fraud or misrepresentation is usually treated as a disputed question of fact to be resolved at trial. Thus, a motion for summary judgment was denied where the plaintiff had relied upon oral statements of the defendant that were contradicted by statements contained in the defendant's written circular,[68] and the same result obtained where the plaintiff produced no evidence in support of a claim that the defendant had fraudulently concealed the physical and mental condition of a company's chief executive.[69]

Genuine issues of material fact have been found to exist with regard to a wide range of questions, including whether bondholders had been placed on notice that an underwriter might be involved in misrepresenting how bond proceeds would be used,[70] the materiality of a fact omitted from a press release,[71] whether purchasers of an investment fund relied on an auditor's representation to their detriment,[72] and whether two parties had, or appeared to have, an agency relationship.[73] Questions of material fact were also found to be presented as to whether the purchasers of municipal securities had informed their broker that they wished to make conservative investments,[74] whether a party was actually the owner and holder of a note,[75] and whether the market was sufficiently efficient to transmit information regarding a security where the plaintiff alleged a fraud on the market by the defendant.[76] On the other hand, however, motions for summary judgment are sometimes granted in municipal bond litigation. For example, they have been used to dismiss some of the parties in multi-party bond-related lawsuits, and where the doctrine of collateral estoppel precludes the relitigation of previously determined factual issues.[77] They are also granted where the terms of particular documents are undisputed, and to determine the legal status of particular parties to the suit,[78] and in a number of other circumstances.

Class Actions

Class action lawsuits are often used to test the rights of bondholding claimants in municipal bond actions. In federal municipal securities litigation, the procedural aspects of class actions are governed by both the Federal Rules of Civil Procedure (which apply generally to all class action suits) and the Reform Act (which imposes additional restraints on class actions involving securities).[79]

Federal Rule of Civil Procedure 23(a) imposes four prerequisites that must be satisfied before a court may certify a class action: numerosity, common questions, typicality, and adequacy of representation. The "numerosity" requirement provides that the potential members of a class must be so numerous as to make it impracticable to join them as individual parties. In municipal bond litigation, this requirement is typically satisfied with little difficulty since municipal bonds are frequently owned by a large number of bondholders. Under the "commonality" requirement, a class action must present questions of law or fact that are common to all members of the class. As a general matter, this prerequisite to class certification will be deemed satisfied where the class members are in substantially identical factual circumstances and the questions of law raised by the plaintiff apply to each class member.[80] In municipal securities lawsuits, the commonality question frequently turns on whether or not the investors who constitute the potential class relied to their detriment upon fraudulent statements made by the bond issuer that were uniform or standardized. Thus, where investors rely on a common written document, such as a prospectus, in deciding whether to purchase a bond, they are likely to satisfy the commonality requirement. On the other hand, when plaintiffs allege fraud on the basis of oral misrepresentations, class certification is frequently denied because the members of the purported class are likely to have received individualized communications, which make it appropriate that their claims be separately adjudicated.[81]

The nub of the "typicality" requirement is that the representative plaintiff party's claims must be typical of those of the class as a whole. The representative's claims need not be identical with those of other class members.[82] Instead, there must only be what one court described as a "basic congruence" between the claims and interests of the named plaintiff and those of the remainder of the class.[83] For the most part, typicality is not a barrier to class certification in municipal securities class action suits. To the extent that the issue is raised, it arises in a context where a potential class contains both current bondholders (who may have a particular interest in prospective relief) and former bondholders (who may have a greater interest in receiving compensation for monetary losses that were incurred in the past). Typicality may also be an issue where the named plaintiff has greater sophistication with respect to the municipal securities market than other class members, since that party may be subject to defenses that may not be raised against less savvy investors.

The "adequacy of representation" requirement mandates that the representative plaintiff be able to represent the interests of the entire class in a fair and adequate fashion. To some extent, this requirement overlaps with the typicality requirement, since the representative plaintiff must be able to prosecute the lawsuit as a fiduciary for the entire class.[84] As one court viewed it, the adequacy requirement has three elements: (1) the class representative may not have interests that are antagonistic to those of other class members; (2) he or she must have sufficient interest in the outcome of the litigation to advocate vigorously on behalf of the class; and (3) counsel for the representative plaintiff must be competent, experienced, and qualified.[85]

Rule 23(b) of the Federal Rules of Civil Procedure establishes requirements that pertain after a class has been certified for "maintaining" a class action lawsuit. Under that rule, a class action is maintainable where one or more of three conditions pertain: (1) there is a risk that inconsistent adjudications or different standards of conduct will result from individual adjudication; (2) the defendant has acted in a fashion that makes injunctive or declaratory relief appropriate; and (3) class issues predominate in the lawsuit, and the class action is superior to other methods of adjudication. In practice, each of these conditions provides a basis for maintaining some type (or types) of municipal bond class action lawsuit(s). Actions in which municipal bondholders seek damages for fraud in federal court may be maintained under the first condition; and these kinds of lawsuits may also be based upon the third condition, since many such cases involve a configuration—in which securities holders are widely dispersed but relevant documents and witnesses are located centrally—that is quite appropriately suited to a class action. In contrast, where a class of bondholders seeks declaratory relief with regard to previously issued bonds, or classes of taxpayers or ratepayers seek to enjoin the issuance of an allegedly unauthorized bond issue, a class action is usually maintainable on the basis of the second condition.

In cases where a bond-related class action is maintained based on the third condition (i.e., class issues predominate), the Federal Rules require that all members of the class be afforded "the best notice practicable under the circumstances, including individual notice to all members who can be identified through reasonable effort."[86] This notice requirement, which has been held to be a due process based right,[87] is intended to give individual class members—who will be bound by any judgment in the class action—a fair opportunity to opt out of the class and pursue legal action on their own.

Similarly, Rule 23 provides that a class action may only be dismissed or compromised with court approval and after notice to all class members.[88] The settlement must (in the court's judgment) be fair to all parties and a reasonable disposition of the dispute.[89] The settlement notice must also provide members of the class with adequate information to decide whether to join or object to the settlement.[90] Moreover, that notice should include any and all information that a "reasonable person" would view as material to reaching an informed, intelligent decision as to whether to be bound by the settlement or opt out of it;[91] and it should also note that a portion of the recovery may be used to cover the costs of litigation, including attorneys' fees.[92]

As noted above, the Reform Act supplements the more generally applicable Federal Rules of Civil Procedure by imposing a significant set of constraints on class actions that allege violations of the federal securities laws. This act was intended to reduce the number of securities-based class actions initiated by so-called "professional plaintiffs." It is also meant to limit both the scope of discovery and the awarding of attorneys' fees in such cases. In particular, the Reform Act mandates that a plaintiff who seeks to become a representative party in a securities law violation class action must provide a sworn certification that contains five statements: (1) the plaintiff has reviewed and authorized the complaint; (2) the plaintiff did not purchase the security in issue in order to participate in litigation; (3) an identification of all other securities class actions in which the plaintiff served (or sought to serve) as a representative party during the preceding three years; (4) a summary of the plaintiff's transactions in the security in question over the preceding three years; and (5) a commitment that the plaintiff will not accept any payment beyond his or her pro rata share of recovery in the case.[93]

In addition, after the plaintiff has filed the requisite certification, the Reform Act establishes a procedure for judicial selection of a "lead plaintiff" for the class. Within 20 days following the filing of the complaint, the named plaintiff must provide notice to the entire class inviting any member thereof to serve as the lead plaintiff. That notice must fairly explain the subject matter of the class action, the claims at issue, the identity of the class, the particular securities law violations that were alleged in the complaint, and a disclosure regarding any possible conflicts of interests. The court may refuse to appoint the party giving the notice as lead plaintiff where it deems this notice to be incomplete or inadequate. Following the notice, the named plaintiff who has given it may (and typically does) move to be appointed the lead plaintiff in the case. In deciding that motion, the court must appoint as lead plaintiff the party with the greatest financial interest in the outcome of the lawsuit unless that party does not satisfy the typicality or adequacy conditions set forth in Rule 23 of the Federal Rules of Civil Procedure. The Reform Act accords the person who has filed the complaint and/or moved to be the lead plaintiff a presumption of adequate representation. However, that presumption may be rebutted by a showing that that party will not fairly and adequately represent the interests of the class.[94] Moreover, the act specifically prohibits a person from being a lead plaintiff (or an officer, director, or fiduciary of a lead plaintiff) in more than five securities actions over any three-year period.

The Reform Act further supplements the requirements of Rule 23 of the Federal Rules of Civil Procedure with respect to the notice that must be provided to class members with regard to the proposed settlement of class actions grounded in noncompliance with federal securities law requirements. In such suits, notice of the settlement must contain at least the following five items: (1) the total amount of the settlement to be distributed to class members (expressed both in aggregate terms and on a per-share basis); (2) the amount the plaintiffs would recover if they prevailed fully on all of their claims; (3) the amount of litigation costs (including attorneys' fees) that the settling plaintiffs propose to pay from the settlement fund; (4) the reasons for the proposed settlement; and (5) contact information for attorneys for the representative and lead plaintiffs in the matter.[95]

A few other characteristics of class actions in municipal securities lawsuits also bear mention. First, in both the federal courts and the courts of some states, the court has discretion to divide the proposed class into two or more subclasses that relate to particular issues raised in the litigation. Second, while they are most typically initiated by bondholders, bond-related class actions are occasionally used defensively. Thus, bond-issuing municipalities may bring action against a class of defendants that consists of all holders of the municipal plaintiffs' bonds.[96] Finally, judgments in class actions are binding upon all members of a class that has been certified in the action (unless those class members have specifically opted out of the settlement), even where those parties have been completely inactive in the litigation.[97] Thus, the notice requirements imposed under state and federal law receive considerable attention and emphasis for the courts before which municipal securities bond actions pend.

Discovery

In the federal courts, as well as the courts of most states, parties are permitted to discover information "regarding any unprivileged matter that is relevant to any party's claim or defense and proportional to the needs of the case."[98] The decision as to what information is "relevant" is generally left to the trial court; and most courts have construed the concept of relevance quite broadly so as to narrow the disputed issues and eliminate surprise cases before them.[99] Nonetheless, trial courts tend to differ in the extent to which the court will impose sanctions for noncompliance with discovery rules, and in their relative willingness to pressure parties to proceed with discovery at a prompt pace. In the federal courts, Rule 26 of the Federal Rules of Civil Procedure establishes a framework for the discovery process. The rule requires the attorneys for the parties to meet "as soon as practicable" to arrange for the exchange of discovery materials (including electronically stored information) and to develop a discovery plan.[100] Within 14 days following that meeting, the parties must provide each other with at least five items: (1) the name, address, and telephone number of each individual likely to have discoverable information; (2) the subject of the information held by each identified individual; (3) a copy of all relevant documents (including electronic documents) and tangible things, or a description and indication of the location of those items; (4) a computation of damages (with supporting evidentiary material, including documents); and (5) any insurance agreement relevant to the claims in the case.[101]

In federal municipal securities cases, expert witnesses are often called at trial to testify as to a wide range of topics—from predictions of damage amounts to the feasibility of construction projects. It is thus significant in this context that parties to federal suits are required to disclose the identity of their own experts who will testify at trial, and the contents of reports that those experts prepare, at least 90 days prior to trial.[102] Moreover, at least 30 days before trial, each of the parties must divulge the specific experts whose testimony they expect to offer in the trial,[103] along with the names and addresses of all other witnesses they will or may call at trial, the identity of each document they will introduce in evidence, and all witnesses whose testimony will be presented by deposition.[104]

As a general matter, in federal cases, a party is permitted to proceed with discovery during the time that a dispositive motion by its adversary is pending before the court. In private lawsuits alleging violations of the federal securities laws, however, a different rule applies. Under the Reform Act, all discovery and other proceedings must be stayed, and the parties have an affirmative obligation to preserve all evidence, while a motion to dismiss is pending.[105] Within the court's discretion, this stay may be lifted, and particularized discovery may be permitted where such narrow discovery is necessary to prevent "undue prejudice." The latter term has been interpreted to mean that, absent discovery, the defendant would be likely to avoid liability.[106]

Four types of discovery are generally permitted in litigation: written interrogatories, inspection and copying of documents and things, depositions, and requests for admissions. Interrogatories are written questions submitted to an adversary party. They are most often used to obtain general information—such as an adversary's contentions, the dates and times of particular events, the location of documents, and the identities of potential witnesses—as opposed to such specific information as the contents of communications and detailed accounts of events. In the federal courts, parties are permitted (as a matter of right) to serve up to 25 interrogatories, including subparts, upon opposing parties. They may exceed that number only with the court's permission or by stipulation of the parties.[107] Once served with a set of interrogatories, a party has up to 30 days to respond or object to them.[108] In instances where the burden of deriving or ascertaining the information requested is substantially the same for the party serving the interrogatory as for the party served, the served party may answer by designating business records that contain the information asked for (including electronically stored records). The party that served the interrogatories must then be afforded a "reasonable opportunity" to examine, audit, or inspect the records that have been identified.[109]

Municipal bond cases are often factually complex and document-intensive. For that reason, discovery by the production and inspection of documents and things in such suits is often both an arduous process and of considerable importance. In the federal courts, the rights of parties to inspect and copy each other's documents and other things is governed by Rule 34 of the Federal Rules of Civil Procedure. That rule permits parties to enter upon one another's land or property for inspection purposes, and it broadly defines "documents" to include writings, graphs, charts, drawings, photographs, computer disks, and any other information that is stored electronically.[110] Where a party wishes to inspect another party's documents, it must serve a written request upon its adversary, describing with reasonable particularity the documents to be inspected. Within 30 days, the served party must respond to the request in writing stating that it will permit the inspection, or objecting upon a stated basis (e.g., burden and expense, irrelevance of the documents sought to the issues raised in the case, vagueness or ambiguity of the request, etc.).[111] Where an inspection of electronically stored information is requested, the requesting party is permitted to "test or sample" the information in question to learn what it consists of, the costs that would be entailed in obtaining all of it, and how valuable it may be to the litigation.[112]

A deposition is the sworn testimony of a witness, given out of court, in response to oral questions propounded by counsel. In the federal courts, parties to lawsuits are limited to ten depositions apiece in the absence of a stipulation. These must be conducted before a notary public or another person with the authority to administer oaths,[113] and the testimony must be recorded by a stenographer or by audiotape or videotape.[114] Individual depositions may not exceed one day of seven hours—computed as the actual amount of time that the witness responds to questions (excluding all recesses and breaks)—unless otherwise agreed to by the parties or ordered by the court.[115] Attorneys representing deponents are entitled to raise objections to the questions asked in depositions. However, those objections must be stated "concisely," and in a "non-argumentative and nonsuggestive manner."[116]

In federal municipal securities lawsuits—as in all litigation in federal court—parties are permitted to notice the deposition of a public or private corporation, and to describe the subject matter on which they seek testimony. Upon receipt of such a notice, unless the party seeking the deposition can show that the deposition of a high-ranking corporate official is indispensable to obtain relevant information, the corporate entity receiving the notice must designate and prepare for deposition a witness to testify on its behalf who has knowledge of the matters described in the notice. That witness may be one of the corporation's agents, employees, officers or directors, or else another person with the appropriate knowledge.[117] In addition to being tools of discovery that are widely used in bond-related (and other) litigation, depositions may be used at trial in lieu of a live witness where one or more of the following conditions are satisfied: (1) the witness is dead; (2) the witness is located more than 100 miles from the courthouse; (3) the witness is unable to attend the trial due to age, illness, infirmity, or imprisonment; (4) the party offering the deposition has not been able to compel the witness's attendance at the trial by subpoena; or (5) other exceptional circumstances exist.[118] Depositions may also be introduced in evidence at trial to impeach the testimony of a witness.[119]

Requests for admission are a discovery tool that is most often used toward the conclusion of pretrial discovery to establish uncontested facts in the dispute. In municipal securities cases, they typically concern such noncontroversial matters as the dates and amounts of trades in particular bonds or the genuineness of relevant documents such as prospectuses, confirmation slips, or accounting statements. Rule 36 of the Federal Rules of Civil Procedure requires that parties serve requests for admission upon their adversaries in written form. Parties who receive such requests must make a reasonable inquiry into the facts. They must then respond by either making the admission requested, denying the request, or objecting by indicating grounds on which no admission or denial can be made. The rule further provides that in the event that the party responding to the request fails to follow the prescribed procedure, the matter on which admissions are requested may be deemed admitted.[120]

Trial

A trial is a formal, adversarial proceeding in which evidence is presented, facts are found, and legal claims are determined. In nonsettled municipal bond lawsuits, trials tend to be limited to actions based upon theories of fraud, or securities fraud. Most other nonsettled litigated bond cases are resolved by motions for summary judgment. The Seventh Amendment to the U.S. Constitution guarantees a right to trial by jury in actions that are known at common law. These clearly include contract and tort actions based upon municipal bonds. It is also well established that plaintiffs are entitled to a jury trial in actions based upon violations of federal securities law.[121] Conversely, however, there is no right to a jury trial in bond-related actions in which the relief sought is an injunction or a declaratory judgment.

The question of whether to seek a jury trial in municipal securities cases is a strategic one. Among the factors to be considered is the possibility that jurors may be biased for or against the municipal party in the case or for or against high elective or appointive municipal officials in the case (particularly if the jurors are taxpayers or residents of the municipality). Other pertinent factors include the likely length of the trial and the technical complexity of the factual issues—which may be difficult for lay jurors to comprehend.

Municipal finance trials often involve complex factual disputes and a multitude of documents. Expert witness testimony is often introduced with respect to such varied subjects as municipal bond market conditions, engineering aspects of bond-financed projects, state substantive law, tax law, and damages. Under the Federal Rules of Evidence, federal courts must apply certain tests in deciding whether to admit expert testimony. Specifically they must determine (1) whether the expert testimony is based on sufficient facts and data; (2) whether the testimony is the product of reliable principles and methods; and (3) whether the witness has applied the principles and methods to the facts of the case in a reliable way.[122] Trial judges have broad discretion to admit or reject expert testimony. The U.S. Supreme Court has made clear that trial courts are to serve as a "gatekeeper" by making certain that "an expert, whether basing testimony upon professional studies or personal experience, employs in the courtroom the same level of intellectual rigor that characterizes the practice of an expert in the relevant field."[123]

In many municipal bond case trials, a party will move for judgment as a matter of law—either at the close of the adversary party's evidence or at the completion of all evidentiary showings. The premise of that motion is that there is no legally sufficient evidentiary basis for the finder of fact to find in favor of the nonmoving party, and that the movant is legally entitled to judgment based upon the facts adduced.[124] In ruling on such a motion, the court must view the facts in favor of the nonmoving party, and it must grant that party all reasonable inferences.

Remedies

As noted above, municipal bond-related lawsuits are often based upon theories of fraud or securities fraud, or on the assertion that a municipality that is planning to issue bonds lacks the legal authority to do so. The plaintiffs in such actions typically seek one or more types of relief, including damages for pecuniary losses, a writ of mandamus, an injunction against the issuance of bonds, or a declaratory judgment. Damage actions based upon fraud usually allege that misleading statements were made in the course of the transactions that preceded the issuance of bonds or that those who participated in issuance of the bonds knew about unfavorable facts but concealed those facts from bond purchasers. These suits may be pursued directly against the municipality that issued the bonds and its responsible officials. They may also seek compensation from other parties involved—such as brokers, accountants, rating agents, and bond counsel—particularly where doctrines of sovereign immunity bar relief against local entities or officials.

In the event of a bond default, judgments may often be obtained directly against the municipal bond issuer. Nonetheless, it has long been established that because municipal funds are held in trust for the public, and for the accomplishment of publicly beneficial purposes, the remedies of garnishment, attachment, and levy may not be exercised against municipal defendants.[125] Moreover, punitive damages may also not generally be obtained against a municipality.[126]

A writ of mandamus is a type of judicial order that compels a public official to carry out a specific act that he or she is legally obligated to carry out. It is an extraordinary remedy, only available when the act in question is ministerial, as opposed to discretionary, and when the public official's duty to act is clear and unequivocal. In municipal bond cases, a writ of mandamus may be used to compel such actions as the collection of taxes to pay a court judgment,[127] the collection of taxes to pay off bonds,[128] the imposition of special assessments,[129] and the establishment of tolls and tariffs on a bond-funded public works project. The issuance of a mandamus writ may be defeated, however, by the existence of legal limits on a municipality's power to tax,[130] or by the resignation of the public official who has been sued.[131]

In other cases, taxpayers, ratepayers, or other interested parties may seek an injunction to prevent the issuance of municipal bonds. A court will grant injunctive relief where the plaintiff can demonstrate that the bonds would be invalid because they are in excess of the authorized amount for such bonds, because their issuance is not for a public purpose, because they were not approved in an appropriate election, or for any other similar reason. Injunctive relief may be denied, however, on the basis of laches or an applicable statute of limitations,[132] or because the court's power to order relief against elected local officials is limited by considerations of the separation of powers.[133]

Finally, as noted previously, bondholders or taxpayers may bring suit for a declaratory judgment invalidating a proposed set of municipal bonds. Such an action asks a court to formally determine the rights and obligations of the parties. It is often accompanied by a request for an injunction against issuance of the bonds in question. As observed previously, however, where such declaratory and/or injunctive relief is sought, the plaintiff has no constitutional right to a trial by jury.

Notes

1. The authors acknowledge their intellectual debt to W. Michael Gamer, whose excellent Chapter 14 in *State and Government Debt Financing* (M.D. Gelfand ed., West Group 1986) provided a good deal of the material for the analysis that follows. We are also grateful to Professor Michael J. Dale of Nova Southeastern University College of Law, who graciously and generously shared with us his expertise in the law of civil procedure.
2. *See* Advisory Commission on Intergovernmental Relations, City Financial Emergencies: The Intergovernmental Dimension (1973); James E. Spiotto, *A History of Modern Municipal Defaults*, *in* The Handbook of Municipal Bonds (Sylvan G. Feldstein & Frank J. Fabozzi eds., John Wiley & Sons 2008).
3. *See* 15 U.S.C. § 78C(a)(2).
4. *Id.* § 78C(a)(12).
5. *Id.* §§ 77–80.
6. *Id.* § 78C(a)(9).

7. *Id.* § 78o-4.
8. Fed. R. Civ. P. 12(b)(1).
9. 28 U.S.C. § 1331.
10. *Id.* § 1332.
11. *See* Morgan's Heirs v. Morgan, 15 U.S. 290 (1987).
12. Strawbridge v. Curtiss, 7 U.S. 267 (1806).
13. Moor v. Alameda County, 411 U.S. 693 (1973).
14. 28 U.S.C. § 1332(c).
15. *See, e.g.*, Curb & Gutter Dist. No. 37 of City of Fayetteville v. Parrish, 110 F.2d 902 (8th Cir. 1940).
16. 28 U.S.C. § 1967(a).
17. *See* MCI Telecomms. Corp. v. Teleconcepts, Inc., 71 F.3d 1086 (3d Cir. 1995).
18. 28 U.S.C. § 1367(c).
19. 18 U.S.C. § 1961 *et seq.*
20. 28 U.S.C. § 1367(b).
21. Mullane v. Central Hanover Bank & Trust Co., 399 U.S. 306 (1950).
22. *See* Int'l Shoe Co. v. State of Washington, 326 U.S. 310 (1945); Shaffer v. Heitner, 433 U.S. 186 (1977); Kulko v. Superior Court of Cal., 436 U.S. 84 (1978).
23. Burger King Corp. v. Rudzewicz, 471 U.S. 462 (1985).
24. *See* 15 U.S.C. § 774; 18 U.S.C. § 1965(a).
25. Fed. R. Civ. P. 4(k)(2).
26. 28 U.S.C. § 1391(a).
27. *Id.*
28. *Id.* § 1391(c).
29. Butterworth v. Hill, 114 U.S. 128 (1885).
30. 15 U.S.C. § 78aa.
31. *See, e.g.*, Chambliss v. Coca-Cola Bottling Corp., 274 F. Supp. 401 (E.D. Tenn. 1967), *aff'd*, 414 F.2d 256 (6th Cir. 1969).
32. Fed. R. Civ. P. 12(b)(3).
33. 28 U.S.C. § 1404(a).
34. *Id.* § 1407.
35. *See, e.g.*, *In re* Capital Underwriters, Inc. Sec. Litig., 464 F. Supp. 955 (J.P.M.L. 1979).
36. *See* Dixie Elec. Co-op v. Citizens of State of Ala., 789 F.2d 852 (11th Cir. 1986).
37. Harris Trust & Sav. Bank v. E-II Holdings, Inc., 926 F.2d 636 (7th Cir. 1991).
38. Lake Carriers Ass'n v. MacMullan, 406 U.S. 498, 506 (1972).
39. *See, e.g.*, City of Philadelphia v. Sec. & Exch. Comm'n, 434 F. Supp. 281 (E.D. Pa. 1977); Atl. Richfield Co. v. FTC, 546 F.2d 646 (5th Cir. 1977).
40. *City of Philadelphia*, 434 F. Supp. 281.
41. Sosna v. Iowa, 419 U.S. 393 (1975).
42. Worth v. Seldin, 422 U.S. 490 (1975); Ass'n of Data Processing Servs., Inc. v. Camp, 397 U.S. 150 (1970).
43. *See, e.g.*, Burks v. Yarbrough, 157 S.W.3d 876 (Tex. App. 2005).
44. Bell v. City of Kellogg, 922 F.2d 1418 (9th Cir. 1991); Posterna v. Snohomish County, 922 P.2d 176 (Wash. Ct. App. 1996).

45. *See, e.g.*, Scachitti v. UBS Fin. Servs., 831 N.E.2d 544 (Ill. 2005).
46. R.R. Comm'n of Tex. v. Pullman Co., 312 U.S. 496 (1941).
47. Burford v. Sun Oil Co., 319 U.S. 315 (1943).
48. Younger v. Harris, 401 U.S. 37 (1971).
49. *See, e.g.*, Chem. Bank v. City of Bandon, 562 F. Supp. 704 (D. Or. 1983).
50. City of Springfield v. Wash. Pub. Power Supply Sys., 752 F.2d 1423 (9th Cir. 1985).
51. Smith v. Travis County Educ. Dist., 791 F. Supp. 1170 (W.D. Tex. 1992).
52. *Id.*
53. *Id.*
54. *See* Bell Atl. Corp. v. Twombly, 550 U.S. 544 (2007).
55. *See, e.g.*, Commander Oil Corp. v. Barlo Equip. Corp., 215 F.3d 321 (2d Cir. 2000).
56. 15 U.S.C. § 178u-4(b).
57. *See, e.g.*, Bankers Trust Co. v. Old Republic Ins. Co., 959 F.2d 677 (7th Cir. 1992).
58. 15 U.S.C. § 78u-4(b).
59. *Compare In re* Silicon Graphics Inc. Sec. Litig., 183 F.3d 970 (9th Cir. 1999) (stating that in 10b-5 action plaintiff must show deliberately reckless or conscious misconduct strongly suggesting actual intent to defraud), *with In re* Comshare Inc. Sec. Litig., 183 F.3d 542 (6th Cir. 1999) (requiring demonstration of facts giving rise to strong inference of negligence); Nathanson v. Zonagen, Inc., 267 F.3d 400 (5th Cir. 2001) (finding that plaintiffs must plead specific facts giving rise to strong inference of scienter); Fla. State of Admin. v. Green Tree Fin. Corp., 270 F.3d 645 (8th Cir. 2001) (holding that plaintiff must demonstrate unusual or heightened motive); Press v. Chem. Inv. Servs. Corp., 166 F.3d 529 (2d Cir. 1999) (stating that plaintiff must show either defendant had motive and opportunity for fraud or strong circumstantial evidence of scienter or recklessness).
60. *See, e.g.*, *In re* Stratosphere Corp. Sec. Litig., 1 F. Supp. 2d 1096 (D. Nev. 1998).
61. *See, e.g.*, Kalnit v. Eichler, 85 F. Supp. 2d 232 (S.D.N.Y. 1999).
62. *See Stratosphere Corp. Sec. Litig.*, 1 F. Supp. 2d 1096.
63. 15 U.S.C. §§ 77z-2, 78u-5. *See, e.g.*, *In re* Advanta Corp. Sec. Litig., 180 F.3d 525 (3d Cir. 1995).
64. *See, e.g.*, Hoeppner v. Crotched Mountain Rehab. Ctr., Inc., 31 F.3d 9 (1st Cir. 1994).
65. Rivera-Muriente v. Agosto-Alicia, 959 F.2d 349 (1st Cir. 1992).
66. Fed. R. Civ. P. 56(a).
67. *Id.* 56(d).
68. Kennedy v. Josephal & Co., Inc., 814 F.2d 798 (1st Cir. 1987).
69. Kazs v. Fin. Gen. Bankshares, Inc., 796 F.2d 508 (D.C. Cir. 1986).
70. *In re* Heritage Bond Litig., 289 F. Supp. 2d 1132 (C.D. Cal. 2003).
71. SEC v. Autocorp Equities, Inc., 292 F. Supp. 2d 1310 (D. Utah 2003).
72. Cromer Fin., Ltd. v. Berger, 245 F. Supp. 2d 552 (S.D.N.Y. 2003).
73. *Id.*
74. Wyman v. Prime Discount Sec., 819 F. Supp. 79 (D. Me. 1993).
75. FDIC v. Selaiden Builders, Inc., 973 F.2d 1249 (5th Cir. 1992).
76. Simpson v. Specialty Retail Concepts, 823 F. Supp. 353 (M.D.N.C. 1993).

77. Miskin v. Ageloff, 299 F. Supp. 2d 249 (S.D.N.Y. 2004).
78. Howard v. Malcolm, 658 F. Supp. 423 (E.D.N.C. 1987).
79. Notably, the Class Action Fairness Act of 2005, which makes a number of changes in the federal procedures governing many class actions, excludes from its coverage class actions that relate to securities. *See* 28 U.S.C. § 1332(d)(9)(C).
80. *In re* Amerifirst Sec. Litig., 139 F.R.D. 423 (S.D. Fla. 1991).
81. Seiler v. E.F. Hutton & Co., Inc., 102 F.R.D. 880 (D.N.J. 1984).
82. *See, e.g., In re* Scott Paper Co. Sec. Litig., 142 F.R.D. 611 (E.D. Pa. 1992).
83. Mobley v. Acme Mkts., Inc., 473 F. Supp. 851, 858 (D. Md. 1978).
84. Christman v. Brauvin Realty Advisors, Inc., 191 F.R.D. 142 (N.D. Ill. 1999).
85. *Id.*
86. Fed. R. Civ. P. 23(b).
87. Carter v. Newsday, Inc., 76 F.R.D. 9 (E.D.N.Y. 1976).
88. Fed. R. Civ. P. 23(e).
89. Teachers Ins. & Annuity Ass'n of Am. v. Beame, 67 F.R.D. 30 (S.D.N.Y. 1975).
90. Oswald v. McGarr, 620 F.2d 1190 (8th Cir. 1978).
91. Phillips Petroleum Co. v. Shutts, 472 U.S. 797 (1985).
92. McCarthy v. Paine Webber Group, Inc., 164 F.R.D. 309 (D. Conn. 1995).
93. 15 U.S.C. § 78 u-4(a).
94. Fischler v. AmSouth Bancorp, 1997 WL 118429 (M.D. Fla. 1997).
95. *See* 15 U.S.C. §§ 772-1(a)(7), 78u-4(a)(7).
96. *See, e.g.*, Marchwinski v. Oliver Tyrone Corp., 81 F.R.D. 487 (W.D. Pa. 1979); Lynch Corp. v. MII Liquidating Co., 82 F.R.D. 478 (D.S.D. 1979).
97. *See, e.g.*, Folding Cartons, Inc. v. Am. Can Co., 79 F.R.D. 698 (N.D. Ill. 1978).
98. Fed. R. Civ. P. 26(b)(1).
99. *See, e.g.*, Heathman v. U.S. Dist. Court for Cent. Dist. of Cal., 503 F.2d 1032 (9th Cir. 1974); Walsh v. Chittenden Corp., 799 F. Supp. 405 (D. Vt. 1992) (finding that public interest in disclosure outweighs need for secrecy).
100. Fed. R. Civ. P. 26(f).
101. *Id.* 26(a).
102. *Id.* 26(a)(2).
103. *Id.*
104. *Id.* 26(a)(3).
105. 15 U.S.C. § 78u-4(b)(3)(B).
106. *See, e.g.*, Global Intellicom, Inc. v. Thomas Kernaghan & Co., 1999 WL 223158 (S.D.N.Y. 1999); Dartley v. Ergobilt, Inc., 1998 WL 792500 (N.D. Tex. 1998).
107. Fed. R. Civ. P. 33(a).
108. *Id.* 33(b).
109. *Id.* 33(d).
110. *Id.* 34(a).
111. *Id.* 34(b).
112. *Id.* 34(a).
113. *Id.* 28(a)(1).
114. *Id.* 30(b)(3).

115. *Id.* 30(d)(1).
116. *Id.* 30(c)(2).
117. *Id.* 30(b)(6).
118. *Id.* 32(a)(3).
119. *Id.* 32(a)(1).
120. *Id.* 36.
121. *See, e.g.*, Mintz v. Allen, 45 F.R.D. 35 (S.D.N.Y. 1968).
122. Fed. R. Evid. 702.
123. *See* Daubert v. Merrell Dow Pharms., Inc., 509 U.S. 579 (1993); Kumho Tire Co., Ltd. v. Carmichael, 526 U.S. 137 (1999).
124. Fed. R. Civ. P. 42.
125. *See, e.g.*, W.K. Terry & Co. v. Hyde County, 168 N.E. 562 (Ohio 1929); Payton v. City of Highland Park, 536 N.W.2d 285 (Mich. 1995); City of Coral Gables v. Hepkins, 144 So. 385 (Fla. 1932).
126. City of Newport v. Fact Concerts, Inc., 453 U.S. 247 (1981); Feingold v. S.E. Pa. Transp. Auth., 517 A.2d 1270 (Pa. 1986).
127. King v. United States *ex rel.* Tiedke, 100 F.2d 797 (5th Cir. 1939).
128. Zelenka v. Wayne County Corp. Counsel, 372 N.W.2d 356 (Mich. 1985).
129. City of Winter Haven v. Summerlin, 154 So. 864 (Fla. 1934).
130. State v. City of Clearwater, 169 So. 602 (Fla. 1936).
131. Yost v. Dallas County, 236 U.S. 50 (1915).
132. *See, e.g.*, Henning v. Town of Sulphur, 186 So. 845 (La. 1934); Gentry v. Taylor, 5 S.E.2d 857 (S.C. 1939).
133. *See, e.g.*, Missouri v. Jenkins, 495 U.S. 33 (1990).

Index